What Does
the Bible
Say About...

Creation

"What Does the Bible Say About...?" Series
Ronald D. Witherup, PSS
Series Editor

Published volumes:

Angels and Demons
John Gillman and Clifford M. Yeary

Animals
Jaime Waters

Education
Allison Gray

Forgiveness
Mary Ann Getty

Friendship
Laurie Brink, OP

Good and Evil
Michael Patella, OSB

Inclusion
Don Senior

Life and Death
John Gillman

Old Age
Ronald D. Witherup, PSS

Slavery and Freedom
Catherine Upchurch

Strangers, Migrants, and Refugees
vănThanh Nguyễn, SVD

Women and Men
John and Florence Gillman

What Does the Bible Say About...?

Creation

David G. Monaco

NEW CITY PRESS
Enkindling the Spirit of Unity

Published in the United States by New City Press
136 Madison Avenue, Floors 5 & 6, PMB #4290
New York, NY 10016
www.newcitypress.com

©2025 David G. Monaco

What Does the Bible Say About Creation?
David G. Monaco

Cover design and layout by Miguel Tejerina

Biblical citations are taken from the *New Revised Standard Version* ©1989 Division of Christian Education of the National Council of the Churches of Christ in the United States of America.

Library of Congress Cataloging-in-Publication Data

Library of Congress Control Number: 2024945292

ISBN: 978-1-56548-657-7 (paper)
ISBN: 978-1-56548-662-1 (e-book)
ISBN: 978-1-56548-697-3 (series ISBN)

Printed in the United States of America

Contents

Series Preface 7

Introduction 9

Chapter One
"Have Dominion" or "Subdue"?:
A Problem of Interpretation 13

Chapter Two
"For the Beauty of the Earth":
The True Meaning of Ecology 26

Chapter Three
Beauty Marred: Consumerism Unleashed 39

Chapter Four
Danger Ahead:
The Controversy over Climate Change 52

Chapter Five
A Planetary Challenge:
Going Green for the Blue Planet 66

Chapter Six
Lessons from a Pandemic 76

Chapter Seven
Stewards of Creation 88

Afterword 101

Notes 105

Series Preface

The Bible remains the world's number one best-seller of all time. Millions of copies in more than two thousand languages and dialects are sold every year, yet how many are opened and read on a regular basis? Despite the impression the Bible's popularity might give, its riches are not easy to mine. Its message is not self-evident and is sometimes hard to relate to our daily lives.

This series addresses the need for a reliable guide to reading the Bible profitably. Each volume is designed to unlock the Bible's mysteries for the interested reader who asks, "What does the Bible say about…?" Each book addresses a timely theme in contemporary culture, based upon questions people are asking today, and explaining how the Bible can speak to these questions as reflected in both Old and New Testaments.

Ideal for individual or group study, each volume consists of short, concise chapters on a biblical theme in non-technical language, and in a style accessible to all. The expert authors have been chosen for their knowledge of the Bible. While taking into account current scholarship, they know how to explain the Bible's teaching in simple language. They are also able to relate the biblical message to the challenges of today's Church and society while avoiding a simplistic use of the biblical text for trying to "prove" a point or defend a position, which is called "prooftexting"—an improper use of the Bible. The focus in these books is on a religious perspective, explaining what the Bible says, or does not say, about each theme. Short discussion questions invite sharing and reflection.

So, take up your Bible with confidence, and with your guide explore "what the Bible says about CREATION."

Introduction

Years ago, in Riverdale, New York, I met an older gentleman by the name of Father Thomas Berry, C.P. I found him to be very pleasant and gracious. He lived next door to a large retreat center in a house that was called the Riverdale Center for Religious Research, and I was quite impressed by the library of books that he had collected. Years later, a member of the local community there told me that, had a former China missionary not reinforced the main staircase with concrete, the weight of the books would probably have caused them to crash through the floors. As I got to know Tom and began to hear about him as a leading figure in ecological studies, I wasn't quite sure what to think.

His influence is put into nice perspective by the advertisement from Columbia University Press for the 2019 book *Thomas Berry: A Biography* by Mary Evelyn Tucker, John Grim, and Andrew Angyal: "Thomas Berry (1914–2009) was one of the twentieth century's most prescient and profound thinkers. As a cultural historian, he sought a broader perspective on humanity's relationship to the earth in order to respond to the ecological and social challenges of our times."[1] I personally recall how he spoke of care of the earth, but honestly, his reference to himself as a "geologian" confused me. As a young man in my early twenties, I had not really spent a lot of time thinking about the wider world around me. I had, in my early teens, enjoyed camping out and the whole experience of nature, but the concept of dam-

Introduction

age to such an environment had never really dawned on me, particularly on a more systemic level.

In later years, I became much more conscious of the fact that we, as a human species, have done a great deal of damage to this world in which we live, and that we are continuing to do so. I have traveled over much of the United States, through most of the countries of Europe, and less so in the Middle East, and have found myself disturbed by some of what I have seen. As a biblical scholar, I have a passion for antiquity. Given the years that I lived in Rome near an ancient Roman house, which I frequently visited and which was right under the basilica attached to my home, I have a deep love for archaeological treasures. The pollution in modern cities built over ancient ones, like Rome, London, and Athens, sometimes having devastating effects upon irreplaceable antiquities, has at times shocked me. Seeing the damage done by exhaust fumes to those treasures deeply saddens me. In my years living in Rome, it was painful to see how the stones of the Colosseum had turned almost black in places due to the pollution from cars when they were allowed to circle the structure. It is therefore quite heartening to see the great work that the Italians have done during recent years in cleaning so many of those stones. On a different note, I remember finding myself disgusted when, on one beach in the Middle East, we were told to avoid the water in an area where there was raw sewage leaking directly into the sea. Given my own personal skittishness, I avoided any contact with the water, period. These and similar experiences have opened my eyes to the concerns of a man like Father Tom.

Now, as a student and professor of the Bible, I sometimes ask myself not so much what the biblical authors say about such environmental issues—because the devastating effects on the environment since the time of the Industrial Revolution would have been completely incomprehensible to them—but rather what they *would* have said. While they would probably not have been able to imagine our world as we know it, the basic principles that they teach us have enduring value and can offer us lessons on how to confront the challenges that face us today. It strikes me that there is some reticence, even among believers, to see how the Bible can teach us anything about the environment. Allow me, however, to propose something similar that few would question. The biblical writers could never have imagined the medical advances that we have seen just in the last century alone. Yet most believers would see that these writers' basic insights, guided by the Holy Spirit, are, in fact, a quite good and reliable guide for how we approach these new issues and challenges. I believe that the same can be said regarding biblical insights that can be applied to our care for the earth and all creation. For the authors of the Old and New Testaments, the world was created by God and created good. This insight alone can be a guide for us in this day and age as we face the results of our own misuse of the resources that God has placed at our disposal and strive to cherish and heal that world. So, get your Bibles ready or just read the quotes in the following pages—let's prepare to explore together the insights and teaching that the Bible has to offer about creation.

Chapter One

"Have Dominion" or "Subdue"?: A Problem of Interpretation

A problem? In the text? What would lead me to use such a term to begin our study? When you take a moment to reflect on the beauty of the natural world, what could be problematic—and what could possibly be problematic about the Bible? Before my knees started to give me problems, I was, for a time, an avid skier. While I occasionally enjoyed working up a little speed and even "getting a bit of air" (albeit very little, maybe just an inch or two), my greatest enjoyment was to find myself atop a mountain, pulling off to the side and just looking out at the magnificent beauty of the surrounding area, feeling that clean, crisp air fill my lungs. How can one not be moved? Even in a big city, a proverbial concrete jungle like New York, a city I love given that I come from the area, as one watches people enjoying even the smallest of parks, it is hard to imagine anyone not caring about the beauty of God's created world. This situation is, however, not quite as simple as it may seem, and sometimes, well-meaning people of faith can be a big part of the problem.

Chapter One

Creation Story Number One: The Roots of the Problem

Many, probably most, of us have read or heard the stories from Genesis. Most of us probably first heard them when we were children, and they have become quite familiar. It is often, nonetheless, a bit of a shock even for people familiar with those stories to think it through and to realize that there is not just one but two biblical accounts of God's creation of the world: Genesis 1:1—2:4a and 2:4b–25. We know them well enough to take them for granted as they stand, mistakenly taking them for one continuous story. Both passages may, then, be quite familiar to us, but it is often difficult for people to realize that they conflict in a number of respects.

Scholars reconcile this circumstance by speaking of the chapters as coming from two separate strands of ancient Israelite tradition, dating from separate eras. The first version, it is suggested, comes from Priestly circles (symbolized by "P"), where God is presented as majestic and creates merely by speaking: "Then God said 'Let there be light'; and there was light" (Genesis 1:3). The second version, according to the theory, comes from a tradition called the "Yahwist" (seen by the use of Yahweh as the name for God but symbolized by "J" because of the German spelling of the name), a more colorful version in which God is portrayed as working with hands: "then the LORD God formed man from the dust of the ground, and breathed into his nostrils the breath of life; and the man became a living being" (Genesis 2:7). Both versions

"Have Dominion" or "Subdue"?: A Problem of Interpretation

proclaim the same reality—the creation of the world and of the human person out of divine love—but they do so in clearly different ways.

In the first Creation account, God begins with the creation of the light, then moves on to separating the waters, creating the sky, then creating the dry land and the seas, after which God moves on to vegetation. After this the sun, moon, and stars follow. Next come the sea creatures and birds, then the land animals. Finally, before the Sabbath rest, God creates humankind, male and female, "in our image, according to our likeness" (Genesis 1:26). With that act of creation finished, God moves from seeing that not only all creation was good, to seeing that "indeed, it was very good" (Genesis 1:31). The second Creation account, which we will detail below, proceeds in a completely different manner.

For our purposes here, though, there is one specific passage that merits some reflection and that is really the crux of the issue (italics added for emphasis):

> Then God said, "Let us make humankind in our image, according to our likeness; and *let them have dominion* over the fish of the sea, and over the birds of the air, and over the cattle, and over all the wild animals of the earth, and over every creeping thing that creeps upon the earth."
>
> So God created humankind in his image, in the image of God he created them; male and female he created them.

Chapter One

> God blessed them, and God said to them, "Be fruitful and multiply, and *fill the earth and subdue it; and have dominion* over the fish of the sea and over the birds of the air and over every living thing that moves upon the earth." God said, "See, I have given you every plant yielding seed that is upon the face of all the earth, and every tree with seed in its fruit; you shall have them for food. And to every beast of the earth, and to every bird of the air, and to everything that creeps on the earth, everything that has the breath of life, I have given every green plant for food." And it was so. God saw everything that he had made, and indeed, it was very good. And there was evening and there was morning, the sixth day. (Genesis 1:26–31)

Two key expressions (those italicized) demand clarification. What do "have dominion" and "subdue" actually mean? Here is our problem. According to an online dictionary, the definition of "dominion," in law, is "supreme authority: sovereignty;"[2] while "subdue," in this regard, means "to conquer and bring into subjection: vanquish; to bring under control especially by an exertion of the will."[3] Taken at face value, it can therefore seem as if there are no limits, no controls, no end to what humanity can do with the earth and its resources based on this biblical charge. But this is a misreading of the text. As Pope Francis explains in his 2023 Apostolic Exhortation *Laudate Deum*, "the world that surrounds us is not an object of exploitation, unbridled use and unlimited ambition. Nor can we claim that nature is a mere 'setting' in which we develop our lives and our projects."[4]

Unfortunately, the idea that the Bible grants us unlimited use of the earth is an argument that I, and likely many readers, have heard. I do not mean to imply that people who use this line of reasoning would say that it is our right actively to destroy the world as we know it. Rather, they would view climate activism as a species of fanaticism relying more on human terms and priorities than on God's perspective.

In an article concerning the attitude of some Christians regarding the concept of climate change, *Newsweek* feature writer Kashmira Gander notes:

> Some evangelicals argue that global warming is of little concern when the end times are approaching. Indeed, it could even be proof of it. Bible verses are also pointed to as evidence humans are required to subdue Earth, that God is in control, and global warming is part of His plan. Others see it as a liberal hoax and a means to push folks away from religion towards the government.[5]

The idea that global warming could be seen as a sign of the end times is particularly problematic in that, for some Christians, it would have an eerily "positive" role in bringing on the end of the present age.

Chapter One

The latter point has an additional, though one might say opposite, problematic aspect because there are those who would view such a role through a much darker lens. Lisa Vox, a historian and author of the book *Existential Threats: American Apocalyptic Beliefs in the Technological Era*, notes that "When scientists began sounding the alarm over climate change in the 1980s, conservative evangelicals, who had been somewhat accepting of environmentalism in the 1970s, became convinced that the Antichrist would use the fear of climate change to seize power."[6] Such an attitude would put environmental activism in a decidedly negative light, viewing it, effectively, along the lines of the service of Satan and thus practically "canonizing" the denial that there is any problem whatsoever.

In recent years, I have been impressed with the number of young people from across the political spectrum who have dedicated themselves to advocating for more responsible policies regarding the environment. What is profoundly disconcerting to me, however, is how frequently one finds adults, not, as they should, commending these activists for their energy, enthusiasm, dedication, and the example that they can actually give to us as adults, but rather attacking them in the press or on social media. I find it especially disturbing to see how some of these same adults couch this cavalier attitude toward what we human beings have done to the limited resources of the planet in the above biblical terms of what amounts to a "right" to do whatever we wish precisely because God commanded us to "have dominion" and to "subdue the earth."

The Second Biblical Reflection on Creation

As noted above, the tenor and details of the second Creation account (Genesis 2:4b–25) are quite different from the first. We begin with a stream rising up to water the ground, "then the LORD God formed man from the dust of the ground, and breathed into his nostrils the breath of life; and the man became a living being" (Genesis 2:7). The Hebrew verb for God's action of "forming" is the same one used in the Bible for how a potter works clay. This gives us a beautiful vision in the text of God getting in there with the hands in order to do the work. This tactile sense continues with the amazing image of God breathing "the breath of life" right into the very nostrils of the man.

God then plants a garden in Eden and puts the man there. God makes fruit trees rise up along with the tree of life and the tree of the knowledge of good and evil, which will figure strongly in the third chapter of Genesis from a negative perspective. The man is placed in the garden in order "to till it and keep it" (Genesis 2:15), a text to which we will return shortly. He is also told by God that he may eat the fruit of any tree except that of the knowledge of good and evil. The formation of other living creatures begins in Genesis 2:18, where it is God who notices that the man is in need of a partner. God starts with the animals of the field and the birds, but no partner is found until God places the man in a deep sleep, removes one of his ribs, and creates the woman, leading to the man's words: "This at last is bone of my bones / and flesh of my flesh; / this one shall be called Woman, / for out of Man this one was taken" (Genesis

Chapter One

2:23). The subsequent verse concerning the two becoming "one flesh" will figure in the New Testament in Jesus' teaching on marriage in Matthew 19:5 and in Ephesians 5:31 regarding the exhortation for Christian husbands to love their wives. The account ends with the man and the woman in the garden, naked and unashamed.

As noted above, these two accounts of Creation in the Old Testament differ in details, in tenor, and in approach to the same reality. However, any conflicting sense did not seem to stop the final editors of the Bible from leaving both in as they stand. This may just be a clue as to how to understand appropriately the commands to "have dominion" and to "subdue the earth." The two Creation accounts need to be taken in relation to one another in order to avoid an interpretation that does violence to the fact that this is, regardless of how one understands "have dominion" and "subdue," ultimately God's creation, not ours. Pope Francis puts it beautifully in his encyclical on the environment, *Laudato Si'*:

> Although it is true that we Christians have at times incorrectly interpreted the Scriptures, nowadays we must forcefully reject the notion that our being created in God's image and given dominion over the earth justifies absolute domination over other creatures. The biblical texts are to be read in their context, with an appropriate hermeneutic, recognizing that they tell us to "till and keep" the garden of the world (cf. *Gen* 2:15). "Tilling" refers to cultivating, ploughing

"Have Dominion" or "Subdue"?: A Problem of Interpretation

or working, while "keeping" means caring, protecting, overseeing and preserving. This implies a relationship of mutual responsibility between human beings and nature.[7]

One of the problems with taking an overly literal, fundamentalist view of the Scriptures is that it is too easy to absolutize one text, as some have done with the Genesis commands "have dominion" and "subdue," while not recognizing other texts that would seem to contradict, or at least act as a counterbalance to, those very texts.

This counterbalancing of texts is, in fact, not an uncommon phenomenon in the Old Testament. A good example is the attitude toward certain non-Israelites in the whole sweep of the Old Testament text. In Deuteronomy chapter 23, for example, Moabites and Ammonites would seem to be shut out and denied any possible entry into the community of ancient Israel. Deuteronomy 23:3–6 makes this stance crystal clear:

> No Ammonite or Moabite shall be admitted to the assembly of the LORD. Even to the tenth generation, none of their descendants shall be admitted to the assembly of the LORD, because they did not meet you with food and water on your journey out of Egypt, and because they hired against you Balaam son of Beor, from Pethor of Mesopotamia, to curse you. (Yet the LORD your God refused to heed Balaam; the LORD your God turned the curse into a blessing for you, because

the LORD your God loved you.) You shall never promote their welfare or their prosperity as long as you live.

The entire book of Ruth, though, shows how a loyal and true Moabite woman could not only become a faithful believer in the God of Israel, but, according to the text, also the great-grandmother of King David.

Another example is that of the ancient city of Nineveh. In the Old Testament, the Assyrians are one of the key enemies of Israel. Nahum cries out against Nineveh "Ah! City of bloodshed, / utterly deceitful, full of booty— / no end to the plunder!" (Nahum 3:1). Given that the Assyrians wipe out the northern kingdom of Israel, Jonah's reticence to preach to the Ninevites in the capital city, and his anger at God's forgiveness toward them, is understandable to the ancient reader or anyone familiar with the story. But as I am fond of saying in my classes, this puts the reader in the very unfortunate position of having to make a choice: siding with Jonah or siding with God.

Unfortunately, people have read biblical texts in isolation for a long time and will probably continue to do so, despite what scholars, teachers, or students of the Bible may say. The Bible has been, and continues to be, misused by people who read it inaccurately, pull an isolated quote out of here or there, and conveniently ignore that there are biblical texts that tell of God being almost disgusted by what people have done to each other based on a distortion of the biblical text.

"Have Dominion" or "Subdue"?: A Problem of Interpretation

If we look back just a few centuries in our Christian history, we can think of the concept of the so-called "divine right" of kings and princes utilized to excuse literally any level of barbarity or cruelty. They cited a text like Romans 13:1–2, which reads: "Let every person be subject to the governing authorities; for there is no authority except from God, and those authorities that exist have been instituted by God. Therefore whoever resists authority resists what God has appointed, and those who resist will incur judgment." Or even 1 Peter 2:17, which exhorts, "Fear God. Honor the emperor"—which is particularly interesting as 1 Peter is probably written in a time in which the Christian community has already witnessed imperial persecution.

Those pushing such a perspective were, of course, not acknowledging the more basic rules of treatment of others, scathing prophetic texts against the wealthy and powerful, and texts blasting the elite. The Letter of James is particularly pointed in this regard, as one can see most notably in 2:6, which asks, "Is it not the rich who oppress you? Is it not they who drag you into court?" Or the particularly harsh text in 5:1 which tells the rich to "weep and wail for the miseries that are coming to you." When put into context with the excesses of the Middle Ages, for example, regarding the aforementioned "divine right of kings and princes," one wonders if they had ever even heard of the Letter of James.

Closer to home here in the United States, where it took a brutal and painful Civil War to correct the situation, one thinks of the enslavement of African peoples being justified because of the cursing of the "sons of Ham" in Genesis 9:22–27. The precise line in verse 25 reads "Cursed be Canaan; / lowest of slaves shall he be to his brothers." This comment is all the stranger regarding this argument, as the Canaanites were actually Semites. People were using a distorted reading of historiography as literal history (not to mention ignoring any concept of genetic science) and choosing to ignore totally the reality of respecting the innumerable places in the Old Testament, in particular, and the Bible, in general, that would undercut the whole position on slavery. To give just two examples: Following the command to release a slave after six years of service, we read "And when you send a male slave out from you a free person, you shall not send him out empty-handed. Provide liberally out of your flock, your threshing floor, and your wine press, thus giving to him some of the bounty with which the LORD your God has blessed you. Remember that you were a slave in the land of Egypt, and the LORD your God redeemed you; for this reason I lay this command upon you today" (Deuteronomy 15:13–15). Second, over and against such a barbaric and totally love-deprived institution, Jesus gave a command of love so great as to charge us even to "Love your enemies" (Matthew 5:44).

So, reading texts in the light of others with a different perspective can be quite beneficial and can avoid taking an approach that is too one-sided. In the case of the Creation accounts of Genesis, as Pope Francis notes, reading Genesis chapter 1 in the light of Genesis chapter 2 helps to nurture a greater balance that makes better sense of the commands "have dominion" and "subdue." Taking such a position can help to shift us from viewing the world as ours to use and exploit however we see fit in having dominion and subduing it, to looking at our role as caretakers of God's creation, as responsible stewards of this wonderful world with which God has gifted us.

If we begin to view our role in creation as that of being responsible stewards of God, we can see a whole new world of opportunities opening up, along with a variety of challenges. One dynamic we may overlook that I consider inherent in this concept is the idea that viewing ourselves, as such, enhances our dignity as God's agents. At the same time, though, it is a challenge and a responsibility.

For Reflection:

- How do you interpret the expression "subdue the earth"?
- Based on the Genesis Creation accounts, what should our attitude toward the totality of God's creation actually be?

Chapter Two

"For the Beauty of the Earth": The True Meaning of Ecology

A famous hymn by Folliott Sandford Pierpoint begins, "For the beauty of the earth / For the glory of the skies / For the love which from our birth / Over and around us lies." It is said that Pierpoint wrote the original poem entitled "The Sacrifice of Praise" in 1864 while reflecting on the beauty of the late spring countryside at his home in Bath, England. Given the many summers of research that I have done in the UK, I am quite familiar with the incredible splendor of so many areas of the English countryside. I can, therefore, find it very easy to appreciate how Pierpoint could have been so inspired. The opening lines of his poem practically jumped out at me when I was first considering the topic of this book.

Think of your own experience. Have you ever looked at a natural scene so beautiful, of such splendor, that it couldn't help but move you? While I was doing my undergraduate degree, I worked full-time in the evenings cooking in a restaurant on the Hudson River in the New York area. The head waiter and I got along well, and we would often get into long debates after work about how I could believe in God. Once, after having worked a particularly late

"For the Beauty of the Earth": The True Meaning of Ecology

Saturday night, then having to approve the kitchen clean-up, do food counts and paperwork, he and I were heading to our cars just as the sun was slowly starting to brighten the sky. It made visible the river and the magnificent sheer rock cliffs of the Palisades across the river. He stopped me and said, "Stop, man! Look! Isn't it magnificent? How can anybody look at something so beautiful and not believe in a God? I don't necessarily mean your type of a God. But how can you not believe in a God?" Given our regular conversations, I was really taken aback by what he said, but I could easily see how hard it was not to be deeply moved by the view that was opening up before our very eyes in those early morning hours.

In this chapter, we will take these insights—what inspired Pierpoint, what has moved us, and what struck my old friend so strongly—and look at how the Bible reflects these same sentiments. These teachings will help us to see the true meaning of ecology as not just a science, which of course it is, but in the sense of all things co-existing in their environment. We will examine first how the Bible speaks of the wonders of the created world before moving on in the coming chapters to the challenges that we and our world face. Let us take a pleasant journey through some biblical texts that reflect on the splendor of the created universe with which we have been gifted.

As noted previously, the second Creation account takes place in a garden. The description of this garden in Genesis 2:8–9 is idyllic, the text calling the trees "pleasant to the sight and good for food." Consider, for example, how we use the term "Edenic" to describe a place of unspoiled natural beauty. Even the tree of the knowledge of good and evil that will become a problem for the man and woman is described in 3:6 as "a delight to the eyes." The wondrous future vision of Isaiah 11:6–9 with its similarly idyllic sense, in which all the earth is filled with knowledge of the Lord, has all manner of natural enemies reconcile: wolf and lamb, leopard and kid, calf and lion and fatling, cow and bear, nursing child by the hole of the asp, and weaned child by the adder's den, all in peaceful coexistence. Throughout the Scriptures, one finds many passages that extol and reflect upon the wonders of nature and the created world.

More recently, in his encyclical letter *Laudato Si'*, Pope Francis, reflecting upon the great saint from whom he took his papal name as well as the Bible, has this to say about the created world:

> What is more, Saint Francis, faithful to Scripture, invites us to see nature as a magnificent book in which God speaks to us and grants us a glimpse of his infinite beauty and goodness. "Through the greatness and the beauty of creatures one comes to know by analogy their maker" (*Wis* 13:5); indeed, "his eternal power and divinity have been made known through his works since the creation of the world" (*Rom* 1:20).[8]

"A magnificent book." I find this image particularly apt as we look at what our book of books, the Bible, teaches us about creation.

The "magnificent book" of nature, in its many facets, is reflected throughout the Bible. The book of nature encompasses land, sea, and sky with all their accompanying flora and fauna. The biblical text sees the whole of creation as good. In Genesis 1:31, only when God has finished the work of creation in its totality, do we read that "God saw everything that he had made, and indeed, it was very good." This is an important point. Up until now in the text, God has seen the various created things individually as "good," but once the human creature stands in the totality of the created world, it is no longer "good," but "very good." Likewise, Wisdom 1:14 tells us that God "created all things so that they might exist; / the generative forces of the world are wholesome, / and there is no destructive poison in them, / and the dominion of Hades is not on earth." I find the Greek term (*sōtērioi*) translated as "wholesome" particularly powerful, as it has the nuance of being salvific. What a remarkable biblical view of this "magnificent book" of ours!

One thing that the ancient Israelites were not was a seafaring people. In the Bible, the sea is looked upon with trepidation. It is seen as a powerful force of primordial chaos that could be brought under control and tamed only by God. The Hebrews were not like the Phoenicians, for example, who were skilled navigators around the Mediterranean Sea, particularly for purposes of commerce. Nor were they the Philistines, whose origins would seem to be from the Aegean Sea, as reflected in Jeremiah 47:4, where they are called "the remnant of the coastland of Caphtor," which most likely refers to the island of Crete.

When Solomon builds a fleet of ships in 1 Kings chapter 9, he needs to augment it with sailors from his Phoenician ally King Hiram of Tyre, as we are told in verse 27: "Hiram sent his servants with the fleet, sailors who were familiar with the sea, together with the servants of Solomon." In contrast, Psalm 107:23–30, for example, reflects a sense of panic during a storm at sea, a reaction more consistent with being unnerved by what was feared as strange or mysterious: "They mounted up to heaven, they went down to the depths; / their courage melted away in their calamity; / they reeled and staggered like drunkards, / and were at their wits' end" (verses 26–27). Nonetheless, some passages not only mention the sea and marine animals, but do so in a distinctly positive manner.

Psalm 93, for example, reflecting on God's majesty and power, speaks of the floods lifting up their voice and calls the waves of the sea "majestic" in verse 4. In Matthew chapter 13, the sea (in reality the lake of Galilee) provides a setting for Jesus' teaching. He sits beside the "sea," and when the crowds arrive, he gets into a boat while the people stand on the beach to hear him tell the Parable of the Sower. In another instance, as Paul heads toward Jerusalem, we read in Acts chapter 21 that before he leaves Tyre, the disciples there, along with their wives and children, kneel down on the beach and pray as they bid farewell to Paul in verses 5 and 6. Sea creatures are even called upon to praise God, as in Daniel 3:79, which reads, "Bless the Lord, you whales and all that swim in the waters; / sing praise to him and highly exalt him forever." In the course of Ezekiel's wondrous vision of the new temple, the water that flows from the temple enters "the sea of stagnant waters" and all becomes fresh, while life abounds. We read in chapter 47, verse 9, "Wherever the river goes, every living creature that swarms will live, and there will be very many fish, once these waters reach there. It will become fresh; and everything will live where the river goes."

Despite a lack of comfort with the sea *per se*, water in general in the land of Israel and Judah is a totally different story. I had the incredible privilege of studying there for about two and a half months back in 1987. When we arrived in the Holy Land, to say that it was hot would be the understatement of the year. Part of our studies involved camping out in both the Israeli Negev desert and the Egyptian Sinai Desert. We were constantly moving through archaeological digs, quite often in desert areas such as the site of Qumran at the Dead Sea, where important ancient scrolls had been discovered in 1947. My blood may be 100% Italian, but of my grandparents, I take after the one grandmother who was born and raised higher up on a mountain in southern Italy and despised the heat. While I will admit that the bone-dry desert heat is in some respects less uncomfortable than the high heat and humidity that I experienced while living in Rome, a temperature topping well in excess of 100º Fahrenheit with no shade for relief was not exactly my idea of comfortable.

Modern irrigation in the Holy Land has made the proverbial "desert bloom"; this irrigation is necessary, as

Chapter Two

the climate itself is both hot and dry. Water is the very stuff of life. The percentage of the human body that is water is remarkably high, so we all need to keep hydrated. As we were taught before venturing out into the Negev and the Sinai deserts, one will die a great deal quicker from thirst than from starvation. Given the heat and the fact that it is a heat with very low humidity, we were instructed on how to recognize the signs of dehydration in the human body and told to react accordingly by immediately drinking water. Water, in that ancient world, was precious; rainfall was seen as a blessing. Without water, there was not only the risk of dehydration, but also the danger of starvation from a poor harvest. All of this is reflected in both the Old and New Testaments.

In Psalm 65, the psalmist speaks in wondrous praise for the gift of water. Verses 9–10 note: "You visit the earth and water it, / you greatly enrich it; / the river of God is full of water; / you provide the people with grain, / for so you have prepared it. / You water its furrows abundantly, / settling its ridges, / softening it with showers, / and blessing its growth." Jesus' interaction with the Samaritan woman in John chapter 4 begins with Jesus tired out during the heat of the day and seated at the well. He asks the woman for a drink as she arrives alone at the well in the middle of the day, an unusual time to seek water. The interaction is, of course, far more profound than the woman first realizes when Jesus speaks of "living water." He will eventually lead her to a proper understanding, but her immediate response—"Sir, give me this water, so that I may never be thirsty or have to keep coming here to draw water" (verse

15)—reveals an understandable material desire. The image of water and the quenching of thirst on an eschatological level (that is, dealing with the end times) is also shown in the vison of the new heaven and the new earth in Revelation chapter 21, where the one seated on the throne promises, "To the thirsty I will give water as a gift from the spring of the water of life" (verse 6).

In like manner to biblical reflections on water, a variety of biblical texts also speak of the beauty of the skies and the creatures of the sky. Psalm 68:33–34 praises God as the "rider in the heavens". The author of the book of Sirach observes, "The pride of the higher realms is the clear vault of the sky, / as glorious to behold as the sight of the heavens" (43:1). The author goes on to reflect on the majesty of the sun, the moon, the stars, the rainbow (verse 11 reads "Look at the rainbow, and praise him who made it; / it is exceedingly beautiful in its brightness"), and all of nature in general, concluding with "For the Lord has made all things, / and to the godly he has given wisdom" (verse 33). In the parable of the mustard seed, we hear how once the plant is grown, "the birds of the air can make nests in its shade" (Mark 4:32). Creation provides comfort even for the least of God's creatures.

Pope Francis refers again to his medieval namesake at the start of his exhortation *Laudate Deum* (it is certainly no coincidence that the exhortation was issued on October 4, the feast day of St. Francis of Assisi) in which he reflects the insights of both the saint and of Jesus regarding the creatures of this earth:

> "Praise God for all his creatures." This was the message that Saint Francis of Assisi proclaimed by his life, his canticles and all his actions. In this way, he accepted the invitation of the biblical Psalms and reflected the sensitivity of Jesus before the creatures of his Father: "Consider the lilies of the field, how they grow; they neither toil nor spin, yet I tell you, even Solomon in all his glory was not clothed like one of these" (*Mt* 6:28-29). "Are not five sparrows sold for two pennies? Yet not one of them is forgotten in God's sight" (*Lk* 12:6). How can we not admire this tenderness of Jesus for all the beings that accompany us along the way![9]

The love and respect of St. Francis of Assisi for all animals is well known, but possibly the most famous story is that of his interaction with the wolf of Gubbio, which he tamed with the Sign of the Cross and called "Brother Wolf." It is not without reason that Roman Catholic parishes will often do a blessing of animals (particularly their parishioners' pets) on the feast day of this great saint.

Just as the Bible mentions both water and sky, so too the land of Israel itself is a major theme in the Bible in general, and the Old Testament in particular, and there are many texts that extol its virtues. One of the more famous passages is Exodus 3:8: "I have come down to deliver them from the Egyptians, and to bring them up out of that land to a good and broad land, a land flowing with milk and honey." This image of a land flowing with milk and honey is repeated several times in Exodus and in Leviticus, Numbers, Deuteronomy, Joshua, Jeremiah, and Ezekiel. Above and beyond praise of the land of Israel itself, many passages reference the beauty of the land in general as well as of its many plants and animals.

The harvest of the land was something over which to rejoice, as its lack meant the possibility of starvation. Of the various Jewish feasts, the most joyous was that of Sukkoth, or Booths. It was originally the feast of ingathering or harvest, and as such, was a time of great joy. We see this feast celebrated in a variety of places in the Old Testament; for example, Ezra chapter 3 tells us that "they kept the festival of booths, as prescribed, and offered the daily burnt offerings by number according to the ordinance, as required for each day" (verse 4). In Nehemiah chapter 8, Ezra began to read to the people from the Law on the first day of the seventh month. On the second day, "they found it written in the law, which the LORD had commanded by Moses, that the people of Israel should live in booths during the festival of the seventh month" (verse 14), and so the people keep the festival. "And there was very great rejoicing" (verse 17). In the New Testament, Jesus himself is seen in John chapter 7 ("Now the Jewish festival of Booths was near" [verse 2]) coming up to Jerusalem and teaching during this festival. Such festivals ultimately were a way to honor God's creation and to give thanks to God for it.

As is clear concerning the festival itself as a time of great joy, so too was harvest in general viewed. Isaiah 9:1–7 speaks of the wondrous coming of a future king, noting in verse 3 that "they rejoice before you / as with joy at the harvest." In Jesus' commissioning of the seventy (or seventy-two, as in some texts) disciples in Luke chapter 10, he reflects this idea of the joy of an abundant harvest when he likens their task to a harvest and tells them to "ask the Lord of the harvest to send out laborers into his harvest" (verse 2).

One of the key features of the land is the mountains, which, as with Moses in the Exodus and the experience of Elijah at Mt. Horeb, are frequently seen as special places of communion with God. Psalm 36:6 likens God's righteousness to the "mighty mountains," while Psalm 72:3 prays, "May the mountains yield prosperity for the people, / and the hills, in righteousness." In Ezekiel chapter 36, when the prophet is told to prophesy to the mountains, the Lord says, "But you, O mountains of Israel, shall shoot out your branches, and yield your fruit to my people Israel; for they shall soon come home" (verse 8).

In the New Testament, Jesus teaches from a mountain: "When Jesus saw the crowds, he went up the mountain; and after he sat down, his disciples came to him" (Matthew 5:1). Mark 6:46 (and the parallel account in Matthew chapter 14), and Luke 6:12 speak of Jesus going up a mountain to pray. The very mountains were a sacred place for revelation and for communing with God. In this perspective, we can perhaps appreciate the sentiment of someone like John Muir (1838–1914), the great California naturalist, who pushed for the creation of Yosemite National Park and other wilderness areas out of his admiration for wild nature. Such far-sighted individuals helped to preserve these inspiring sights of nature for all future generations.

Psalm 104 is a hymn of praise to God that reflects on the various wonders of the created world and of its many inhabitants. It speaks of heavenly wonders like the clouds, the winds, the foundations of the earth, the waters. The psalmist speaks of giving drink to the wild animals (verses 10–11), of birds singing from the branches (verse 12), and of God feeding the cattle with grass (verse 14). Verses 16–17 describe the trees as home to birds, while verse 18 tells how "The high mountains are for the wild goats; / the rocks are a refuge for the coneys." According to verse 21, even young lions ask God for their food. The psalm also speaks of the moon and the sun marking times and seasons and the wonders of the mysterious sea, which is "great and wide, / creeping things innumerable are there, / living things both small and great" (verse 25).

All of this we read in our book of books, the Bible, about our other "magnificent book," the beautiful natural world with which we have been blessed. There is so much in nature to excite wonder and admiration, as so many of us know from our own experiences with the marvels of the natural world around us. We see our own thoughts and feelings reflected in the words of the Bible. All aspects of our world are appreciated: sky, earth, oceans and seas, mountains and hills, birds of the air and all kinds of animals, trees and plants, even rocks and stones. All of it is there for our appreciation, if we take the time to notice. There is, however, another side to this praise of creation.

Alongside these more positive reflections, we turn in the next chapter to examine a darker side of human progress and interaction with nature.

For Reflection:

- Have you ever experienced a scene of such natural wonder that you could only look in admiration and silence, contemplating the beauty of God's created world? How has this experience affected your life?

- Does the image of nature as a "magnificent book" make sense to you and, if so, how?

Chapter Three

Beauty Marred: Consumerism Unleashed

The document *Laudato Si'* begins with the words of St. Francis of Assisi and notes that the saint called the earth, our common home, "our Sister." Pope Francis then goes on to say:

> This sister now cries out to us because of the harm we have inflicted on her by our irresponsible use and abuse of the goods with which God has endowed her. We have come to see ourselves as her lords and masters, entitled to plunder her at will. The violence present in our hearts, wounded by sin, is also reflected in the symptoms of sickness evident in the soil, in the water, in the air and in all forms of life. This is why the earth herself, burdened and laid waste, is among the most abandoned and maltreated of our poor; she "groans in travail" (*Rom* 8:22). We have forgotten that we ourselves are dust of the earth (cf. *Gen* 2:7); our very bodies are made up of her elements, we breathe her air and we receive life and refreshment from her waters.[10]

A sad commentary, but unfortunately quite true.

Chapter Three

In most of the places in which I have lived, I am glad to say that I have become accustomed to recycling, including separating types of products, such as paper, plastic, and metal. Nonetheless, even in recent years, I have found myself in places in which I might finish a plastic bottle of water, for example, then ask where I might put my recycling only to be told, "Oh, don't worry about that, just throw it in the trash." When possible, I try to bring empty plastic bottles back with me so that I can at least do my part to keep them out of a landfill. I remember being in one place in which I had been told just to throw away the plastics and then, asking why there was nowhere to put my recycling, was told that it would cost too much to make arrangements for it. Again, a sad commentary. Saving money, it is reasonably safe to say, is generally a positive goal, but in a case like this, at what future cost?

At what future cost? To quote Shakespeare in Act III, Scene 1 of *Hamlet*, "ay, there's the rub." It strikes me that human nature is such that we have the tendency to try to get the most out of the present, which too is just fine in and of itself, but unfortunately, we do not often think of the future. *Carpe diem* ("seize the day") is not necessarily the worst idea in the world—within appropriate limits, of course—but can we justify doing so, or, to put it another way, can we afford to do so when it literally puts later generations at risk? Do we not, rather, bear the weight of some responsibility for those who follow us on this planet?

In 1 Timothy chapter 5, in the midst of a section in which the author gives advice regarding what would seem to be some type of "Order of Widows" in his church community, he teaches that "whoever does not provide for relatives, and especially for family members, has denied the faith and is worse than an unbeliever" (verse 8). Granted, the context is different, but can we not apply this to ourselves and the human family to which we all belong? We have a responsibility beyond ourselves to future generations.

Where to Begin?

Strangely enough, when one speaks of pollution in general, we tend, understandably, to think of what we know from more recent history, and particularly what we see around us. But the origins actually go back quite a bit further than one might think in this day and age. According to Jerry A. Nathanson in the *Encyclopaedia Britannica*'s entry on pollution:

> Pollution has accompanied humankind ever since groups of people first congregated and remained for a long time in any one place. Indeed, ancient human settlements are frequently recognized by their wastes—shell mounds and rubble heaps, for instance. Pollution was not a serious problem as long as there was enough space available for each individual or group. However, with the establishment of permanent settlements by great numbers of people, pollution became a problem, and it has remained one ever since.[11]

In other words, it would seem that we pollute by our very nature as social beings. As this quotation notes, and as any scholar of antiquity would say, archaeological discoveries of such "pollution" as potsherds, for example, are a veritable treasure trove for understanding and dating an ancient site and culture. In fact, the remains of ancient pottery are some of the best indicators for determining the antiquity of an archaeological site. So, from this vantage point, human waste can have a value historically to help describe distant cultures and peoples.

War and conscious destruction cause such levels of ruin much quicker than the natural passage of time would. A good example appears in Nehemiah chapter 4, where we find ourselves in the midst of Nehemiah's attempt to rebuild the walls of Jerusalem that had been destroyed by the Babylonians in 586 B.C. (the destruction itself is detailed in 2 Kings chapter 25 as well as in Jeremiah chapter 39), along with the city as a whole and the Temple in particular. The discouraging lament by the residents of Judah shows how the remains of the destruction, what would qualify by definition as pollution, had been left where they fell: "But Judah said, 'The strength of the burden bearers is failing, and there is too much rubbish so that we are unable to work on the wall'" (Nehemiah 4:10).

The history of diseases borne by filth and human waste is both long and distasteful to consider. This is recognized in Revelation 6:8, in which the rider on the "pale green horse"—Death, accompanied by Hades—is given authority over a quarter of the earth, "to kill with sword, famine, and pestilence." At the same time, however, we now know that "pestilence" can be handled in part by practicing better hygiene. One of my grandmothers was born in the Italian province of Puglia. I have one Pugliese cousin who boasts that Puglia is traditionally a very clean province. I remember driving around the region with him as he waxed eloquent about how Puglia handled the bubonic plague during the Middle Ages better than other parts of the medieval European world, because they took great care to try to keep their cities clean and not let waste pile up. If only it were so easy today! This is certainly a far cry from what is necessary to deal with what we moderns produce in the way of pollution as we know it.

Ratcheting Up the Problem: The Industrial Revolution

So, when did things change to what we, in our modern world, would be more likely to consider "pollution"? When did it shift to more serious and lasting damage to the environment? What moved us as a people from pollution that could be dealt with by changing patterns of hygiene and cleanliness to pollution that does deep and lasting damage to air, water, and land? It certainly did not occur overnight. Nathanson's article points out that the use of coal around the year 1000 A.D. began to really foul the air and that this grew incrementally worse beginning in the seventeenth century with the use of coke (a coal product) for iron smelting. As far back as 1306, King Edward I of England actually enacted what might be one of the first laws concerning air pollution when he forbade the burning of sea coal in London. While

Chapter Three

the fine was "grievous ransom," it was a law that he obviously took seriously, as is evidenced by the fact that one person who broke it three times seems to have been executed for the offence.[12] Did the law really work? Unfortunately, it would seem not, as things grew far worse over time.

In William Blake's poem "And Did Those Feet in Ancient Time." (better known in its later incarnation as the classic English hymn "Jerusalem"), he speaks of the "dark satanic mills." It may be difficult to say exactly what Blake meant by the line, but given the situation of his time, the simplest interpretation would seem to be the industrial factories of the early nineteenth century. One thinks also of the settings of urban squalor and the oppression of the poor during the Industrial Revolution in a fair number of the works of Charles Dickens (1812–1870). The opening paragraphs of *Bleak House* (1853), for example, give a frightening view of the pollution of London at the time. As human technology developed, particularly regarding the use of fuels like coal and coke, pollution levels rose dramatically.

It is the Industrial Revolution, despite the technological advances that it brought (which, I should note, in fairness, are certainly not to be taken lightly), that began to bring into play new forms of pollution of the air, the land, and the water, due to runoff from industrial factories. These newer modes of pollution led to the situation in which we find ourselves today, although in more recent years, we have added new sources for fouling the air and these, unfortunately, have led and are leading to more devastating climactic problems. As the editors of history.com note, what fouls the air most in the present age is something that would have been unimaginable to our forebears, namely the use of motor vehicles. When my grandparents were born, the idea that most families, at least in the Western world, would own at least one car was incomprehensible. But how many families in the Western world today have just one? Add to that the number of buses, trucks, planes, and other vehicles that burn fossil fuels, and, well, you get the picture. These add to greenhouse gases in the atmosphere and thus add to the very serious and devastating problem of climate change, such as global warming and the increased intensity and frequency of severe weather events.[13]

Fortunately, more and more laws have been enacted to try to deal with these problems, despite the fact that we have also seen efforts to undo some of these laws in recent years. The idea that some change is needed, though, seems to be at least generally accepted, as we have learned the hard way in many areas in the world. That is not to say, of course, that there are not people who dismiss or even deny the very problem of pollution. Those who do seem to have a bit of an agenda.

Denial of the problem can undermine efforts to put controls and clean-up protocols into place with the rationale that they would end up cutting into profits. In *Laudate Deum*, Pope Francis comments on one such type of "agenda" and responds with a suggestion to answer any objections:

> It is often heard also that efforts to mitigate climate change by reducing the use of fossil fuels and developing cleaner energy sources will lead to a reduction in the number of jobs. What is hap-

pening is that millions of people are losing their jobs due to different effects of climate change: rising sea levels, droughts and other phenomena affecting the planet have left many people adrift. Conversely, the transition to renewable forms of energy, properly managed, as well as efforts to adapt to the damage caused by climate change, are capable of generating countless jobs in different sectors. This demands that politicians and business leaders should even now be concerning themselves with it.[14]

It would seem, from the pope's comments, that businesses, ironically, might actually be missing out on other means of profit that would come precisely from environmental care.

There are, nonetheless, simply too many examples of environmental problems throughout the entire world to justify an attitude that effectively puts our heads in the sand regarding what is going on around us. One such piece of evidence, a particularly frightening one, is the famed London smog of 1952. Over the course of five days that December, four thousand people died, and it is said that about one hundred thousand were sickened as the skies grew so dark with pollutants that the London buses needed to have their lights on and a guide walking in front of them in order to operate in the daytime.[15] This is not an issue of a simple "pea soup" fog, but rather seems almost apocalyptic in retrospect.

The Lake of Fire

So how about a biblical and apostolic period perspective? Revelation 19:20 describes a "lake of fire" into which the beast and the false prophet are thrown, as are the devil, Death and Hades, and all whose names are not written in the book of life (20:10, 14, and 15, respectively). The idea is probably not meant to be taken literally, but is rather an apocalyptic *topos* or metaphor. It makes me think, however, about very real situations in which more than one body of water has actually caught fire. The WorldAtlas website comments on "Rivers that Have Caught on Fire", a concept almost impossible to imagine, yet sadly true. In addition to the famous case of the Cuyahoga River by Cleveland, Ohio, the site lists five other bodies of water worldwide that have caught on fire, all due to pollution. Four of these are found in the United States, with incidents dating from the late 1800s up to 1969; more recently one river in China (2014) and a lake in India (2015) caught fire.[16]

Less extreme, but also quite disconcerting, is an event that happened to a very good friend of mine who went swimming a few years back in Lake Erie, only to develop cellulitis. Lake Erie today would seem to be far less polluted than it was, for example, in the 1950s and 60s. Nonetheless, the problem has not been eradicated, as my friend found out the hard way. He had a cut on his leg and some residual pollutant in the lake probably infected him through that cut. Cellulitis can easily be treated, but left to itself, it can also be fatal, should it reach the heart. That certainly gives pause for thought.

Chapter Three

All of this is a far cry from the powerful words of the early first-century martyr St. Clement of Rome, who attributes even a maternal sense of care for humanity to the earth's waters. In his Letter to the Corinthians (from around 80–97 A.D.), there is a powerful passage that speaks to this idea:

> The seasons, spring, summer, autumn and winter, follow one another in harmony. The quarters from which the winds blow function in due season without the least deviation. And the ever-flowing springs, created for our health as well as our enjoyment, unfailingly offer their breasts to sustain human life. The tiniest of living creatures meet together in harmony and peace. The great Creator and Lord of the universe commanded all these things to be established in peace and harmony, in his goodness to all.[17]

Not only does Clement see the waters as nurturing us, but he also notes that they are created for our well-being and for "our enjoyment." How sad to reflect on what we have done to so many of those life-giving waters.

Once more, in order to put things into perspective: As human beings in society, we pollute. We have done so from time immemorial. As technologies have developed, though, our levels of pollution and the types of pollutants that we produce have increased and changed, and not for the good. Our desires for the latest goods and conveniences drive the markets. Manufacturers know and rely upon this.

Pope Francis, in *Laudato Si'*, reflects on what he calls a "throwaway culture." A good example of what he refers to is the phenomenon of "planned obsolescence." Years ago, appliances, for example, were made to last. My mother has a refrigerator/freezer in the basement of the house in which I was raised that is closing in on 60 years old and still works perfectly. That is simply not how things are made today. The newer, better units are designed according to planned obsolescence to last a far shorter amount of time so that the consumer will not only want to, but will actually need to, buy another one in the not-too-distant future. What is done, then, with the "obsolete" items? Do we recycle them? Do we leave them off in a dump somewhere?

Even were it not for planned obsolescence, we have what seems to be a natural tendency to always want to trade up for something better and newer. Companies jump on this sentiment and prepare catchy ad campaigns in order to offer more and more new and improved items for sale. The more we desire, the more will be produced, often without any concern for the aftereffects of that production. There is an old expression: "The more things change, the more they stay the same." One thing that stays the same is human nature. When we want something, we do what we can to get it, even if our efforts to fulfill that desire might be at the expense of others.

My paternal grandfather, born and raised in a city just outside of Naples, Italy, was illiterate, but an incredibly wise man. He would often repeat an old Neapolitan expression that is hard to translate, but the basic meaning is of fat choking a person off at the neck. The metaphorical idea is that as people get more prosperous, they don't know when to quit; they want more and more, and can never seem to get enough until they practically choke on it. This dynamic has existed for ages. In the book of Amos, chapter 8, the prophet is dealing with a situation of injustice in the midst of great prosperity in the Northern Kingdom of Israel. The Assyrian Empire, which would soon wipe the Northern Kingdom off the stage of history, was more or less "out of sight, out of mind" for the time being. Everything was about to come crashing down, but in the meantime Amos is faced with the elite who simply can't get enough—and as the prophet points out, their desires come at the expense of the most vulnerable. In Amos 8:5–6 he quotes them: "When will the new moon be over / so that we may sell grain; / and the sabbath, / so that we may offer wheat for sale? / We will make the ephah small and the shekel great, / and practice deceit with false balances, / buying the poor for silver / and the needy for a pair of sandals, / and selling the sweepings of the wheat."

Rampant consumerism has led to a somewhat strange and paradoxical situation. We live in a world in which more and more people are conscious of the problems associated with pollution. We have more laws regulating it now than at any other time in history. Yet, we also find in both society and government a reticence to challenge environmental problems when they might impinge on our needs and desires, particularly in the so-called "developed world," and often at the expense of the "developing world." The argument is often made that the cost of environmental cleanup is too high. Is the cost high? Most certainly. But given the long-term effects, is it not worth it? Or better asked: Can we afford *not* to do it, for the sake of us all? Although the biblical authors were unaware of, and could not foresee, our present rather dire situation, their attentiveness to the poor and needy made them explicitly critical of unconstrained consumerism within limits. Perhaps we need to recapture some of this initiative.

What Next?

In the next chapter, we will examine what strikes me as the most pressing of challenges, and what is probably the more controversial topic: climate change. There, we will look at an issue not so simply "fixed" by regulations, but having a more lasting and devastating effect on us all and upon so many different endangered species of our common home, or as St. Francis would say, of "our (wounded) sister."

For Reflection:

- Have you ever taken the time to consider the negative effects of any of the consumer goods of which you are fondest? What do you think can be done about uncontrolled consumerism?

- Do you know of any places near your home which are particularly polluted? Are you aware of anyone trying to do anything about it? Can you promote some action to remedy the situation?

Chapter Four

Danger Ahead:
The Controversy over Climate Change

Not every problem in life can be "fixed." Some problems are simply beyond our capacity to affect or solve. At the same time, however, human beings have made tremendous strides in confronting difficulties that centuries ago would have seemed to be completely insurmountable. When I worked in the restaurant, as I was working my way up the ladder in the broiler bar, I remember a fellow assistant cook who was older than the rest of us and, as I recall, had served in the Navy during the Vietnam War. He was looking for work (and eventually found it) in aircraft construction. He was a great guy and much missed after he left for California and his dream job, although I was happy for him. His life experience made for many fascinating conversations. I remember one evening, while we were working, when he began to talk about the state of the world and said to me with real passion, "You know what, man? Look at the world. We've got a choice! We can either blow each other up or we can choose to hold hands and shoot for the stars!"

His words really struck me at the time, and I've often reflected on them over the course of the years. "Hold hands and shoot for the stars!" While he did not put it in these terms, his comments emphasize for me a faith-filled perspective that human beings are gifted by God with our intellect and with the capacity to reason things out and seek answers to situations that confuse or trouble us. The scientific progress that we have made and that we continue to make can be used for positive purposes, to better the quality of our lives and to tackle issues that might seem insurmountable and are certainly far beyond what people in ancient times could have even imagined.

When we put our heads together, it is really amazing what we can do. One need only look to how medical advances have cured diseases that were previously seen as incurable. For example, both the Old and New Testaments contain numerous passages referring to leprosy, a disease viewed with particular fear as it entailed separation from the community. To be fair, I should note that despite the use of the term "leprosy," the nature of the disease as we find it described in the biblical texts—particularly the sense that it can be cured naturally—should lead us to realize that the leprosy of the Bible is not exactly what we know today as leprosy, namely the Hansen's disease which took the life of the famed Father (now Saint) Damien of Molokai (1840–1889). As serious as this disease is, though, medical advances have made it such that it is now treatable via pharmaceutical therapies. The research work that made this possible seems to me to exemplify what my friend called "holding hands and shooting for the stars."

Climate change is, admittedly, not something that the Bible addresses directly. Nonetheless, the biblical authors did recognize their vulnerability in the face of natural forces. Drought, famine, floods, and other natural disasters would have been part of their reality despite not realizing how these situations were influenced by the weather and how natural phenomena such as ocean currents impacted the weather. In that sense alone, we can see that weather has always had an influence on our climate, but scientists signal how modern developments such as the use of fossil fuels and practices such as deforestation have greatly exacerbated the situation.

The ancients did not have our scientific knowledge, but they did realize the need to cooperate in order to safeguard resources. Leviticus chapter 25 mandates a type of "Sabbath" for the land every seven years. The Israelites are told that their produce in the sixth year will be sufficient to hold them over for the seventh and until the new crop comes in in the years after. From a practical standpoint, this probably helped to avoid overuse and depletion of the land, although the greater concern in Leviticus is Sabbath rest rather than agricultural utility or necessity. Regardless, one sees a concern for storing up from the prior year. Likewise, in Genesis chapter 41, when Joseph interprets Pharoah's dreams about the fat and thin cows and the plump and thin ears of grain as harbingers of a brutal famine to come, they immediately move to ensure that produce is stored up to protect against the coming famine under Joseph's direction.

When we put our heads together, in fact, we can do amazing things, but what about when we obstruct or undermine one another? Research does not come cheap.

When groups with agendas undermine and cut off funding for research, how are scientists able to make the kind of strides that they could if they had the funding, research tools, and equipment necessary to properly investigate potential solutions and test their results? A good example of this dynamic, it seems to me, is visible in the work being done to confront the larger issue of climate change.

The topic has become quite controversial. Most people recognize the need to control pollutants and counter deforestation, but when it comes to the more direct topic of climate change, there are those who deny the very problem, who look to explain away even the idea that there is anything of real concern regarding climate change. They argue, for example, that any change that we experience is effectively cyclical, that the climate is always changing, or that while there may be a problem, it is not the result of human activity. Some even argue that warming is beneficial to the earth. When large groups of people deny or downplay the problem, pressure can be exerted in order to deny or cut off funds for research designed to confront the issue.

In the article "Climate Change Denial: Facing a Reality Too Big to Believe," two experts try to examine why so many people engage in climate change denial. As the authors note, "Psychologists consider denial—the refusal to accept facts in order to protect us from uncomfortable truths—to be a primitive defense mechanism." In the case of climate change, relying on a defense mechanism is understandable, given that, as the authors note, "The problem is just so huge that it is nearly unthinkable. Our minds try to save us from utter hopelessness by pushing aside thoughts of climate change. Denial kicks in as our minds' default for temporary self-preservation."[18]

Acknowledging the problem of climate change is a challenge to us all, particularly as we look to the future. Again, it is difficult to say what the Bible teaches about the denial of climate change simply because the concept of a human capacity to alter the climate would have been unthinkable to the ancients. Yet we can look at the biblical response to famine, which occurred periodically in the ancient world. People knew to plan ahead and to store up for the future. We can therefore try to look to basic biblical principles that can guide us as we confront this or any issue.

A key principle driven home in both the Old and New Testaments is that we are responsible for one another. No one is, in biblical teachings, a completely isolated individual. Consider Jesus' parable of the rich fool in Luke, where the man is singled out for caring only for himself in the face of an abundant harvest. We read: "But God said to him, 'You fool! This very night your life is being demanded of you. And the things you have prepared, whose will they be?'" (Luke 12:20). Likewise, the Creation accounts in Genesis lay out our role as stewards of God's creation—it is not simply ours to use for our own gain and amusement. It is our responsibility to be good stewards and, as part of that task, not to exploit and deplete all of the world's resources. Responsible stewardship comes from the divine call to safeguard and protect all that with which we have been gifted.

So, while the ancients did not face the problem of irresponsible stewardship at the scope we now do, they did face struggles with doubt about their role and the importance of fulfilling it, and the need to get over that doubt. Getting past denial and trying to tackle the problem, even if it means some sacrifice on our part in the present, could have potential benefits that will never manifest if we refuse to acknowledge the issue such that it only gets worse. This dynamic seems operative to me in biblical texts in which people are called to overcome doubt in order to experience a better and fuller future that they cannot otherwise imagine.

One great problem with doubt is that it can close us off to new and as yet unconsidered possibilities, especially when things look darkest. Isaiah chapter 40 begins "Comfort, O comfort my people, / says your God" (verse 1). It is a passage familiar to many of us from the readings of the Advent and Christmas seasons, so much so that the power of the line as it connects with the remainder of the chapter may escape us. This verse begins the second part of the book of Isaiah, a section following the destruction of Jerusalem and the kingdom of Judah by the Babylonian Empire. It is hard for us to even imagine just how devastating this event was to the ancient Judean people, especially to those who were residents of the holy city of Jerusalem itself. For those who believed that Jerusalem was inviolable because of the presence of the Lord in the Temple, it must have been almost incomprehensible to see both the city of Jerusalem and her Temple destroyed and burned.

Chapter Four

Those who experienced this terrible tragedy and the pain and shock of the Babylonian Exile would have been tempted to abandon hope and give in to despair. Enter the prophet in Isaiah 40:1 (whom we call Second Isaiah), breaking new ground. Earlier prophets had tended to focus on judgment, but now the survivors of the destruction hear stunning words of comfort which continue throughout the chapter. Isaiah 40:27 reflects some of the despair felt by the exiles, the sense that they had been abandoned by a God who no longer cared for them. But the prophet nevertheless emphasizes God's ability to heal and raise up, culminating in verse 31: "Those who wait for the Lord shall renew their strength, / they shall mount up with wings like eagles, / they shall run and not be weary, / they shall walk and not faint."

The same dynamic is operative in the prophet Ezekiel's vision of the dry bones in chapter 37 of his book. The first part of the book of Ezekiel is marked by prophecies of gloom and doom. He drives home a message of destruction and devastation by the Babylonians, but now, after this has all come to pass, the prophet begins to emphasize a new future of hope that must have been difficult for his hearers to even imagine, never mind believe in. Jerusalem is destroyed and they are in exile, but the dry bones are a sign that the Lord will bring about a restoration. The Lord tells Ezekiel to prophesy to the dry bones, that they will have flesh and skin and live; and to the breath, or wind, to come upon the bones and make them live.

> Then he said to me, "Mortal, these bones are the whole house of Israel. They say, 'Our bones

are dried up, and our hope is lost; we are cut off completely.' Therefore prophesy, and say to them, Thus says the Lord GOD: I am going to open your graves, and bring you up from your graves, O my people; and I will bring you back to the land of Israel. And you shall know that I am the LORD, when I open your graves, and bring you up from your graves, O my people. I will put my spirit within you, and you shall live, and I will place you on your own soil; then you shall know that I, the LORD, have spoken and will act, says the LORD." (Ezekiel 37:11–14)

Both in the cases of Second Isaiah and of Ezekiel, the people are called to put aside despair and disappointment and embrace hope and a new future. If they can cast off doubt, they can begin to both experience and work for something new, something that was unimaginable and impossible to any but the Lord.

In the New Testament, the theme of doubt comes up in a variety of ways. People continually doubt the miracles and the identity of Jesus. But I find it particularly powerful when we reflect on doubt regarding the resurrection of Jesus. After two thousand years of history and faith, Christians can forget just how shocking the arrest and death of Jesus must have been to the first disciples, who actually lived through those events. In Jesus, they saw someone who had motivated them to leave their past behind to follow him. Then in a seeming blink of the eye, all came crashing down around them as they had to confront the horrible death that

Chapter Four

he suffered. Keep in mind too, that for his closest disciples, there was a reasonable fear that they could end up as Jesus did if the Romans, who were not exactly the most forgiving of people, were to turn an eye toward them. It must have been demoralizing as they wrestled with fear, grief, and dread, as evidenced in the account of the two disciples on the road to Emmaus (see Luke 24:13–24). Then, seemingly out of the proverbial blue, they hear of his resurrection.

The most famous incident of doubt for Christians is the "doubting Thomas" scene in the Gospel of John. "So the other disciples told him [Thomas], 'We have seen the Lord.' But he said to them, 'Unless I see the mark of the nails in his hands, and put my finger in the mark of the nails and my hand in his side, I will not believe'" (John 20:25). Yet the Gospels of Mark, Matthew, and Luke all reflect doubt also on the part of the disciples regarding the resurrection. A good is example is Matthew 28:16–17: "Now the eleven disciples went to Galilee, to the mountain to which Jesus had directed them. When they saw him, they worshiped him; but some doubted." It is only when they get past their doubt that they are able to embrace the message of hope and move forward into a new future that they never could have imagined before, a future that took them from hiding away in terror in the upper room in Jerusalem (see John 20:19) to becoming bold proclaimers of the resurrection even beyond the boundaries of Israel. What if we were to confront the denial of climate change and embrace the possibility of constructive responses, if we will but commit ourselves to working together—even if that means some sacrifice—for a better future? Can we then, as my old friend would say, "hold hands and shoot for the stars"?

What I am presenting may sound quite naïve, given the scope of the problem. Some might reasonably argue that there is nothing that can be done at this point, and that reaction is certainly understandable—it would be very difficult to ignore the enormity of the problem. But can we really afford literally to sit back and do nothing? Is that being "responsible stewards" of the earth? Should we not be willing to seriously confront the problem with a view to what we are to hand on to future generations? If there is even a chance to do something positive and constructive, is it not at least worth considering regardless of the challenge?

Unfortunately, as noted above, climate change has become a source of some controversy. The United States Conference of Catholic Bishops addressed its reality in their 2001 document *Global Climate Change: A Plea for Dialogue, Prudence, and the Common Good*:

> Responsible scientific research is always careful to recognize uncertainty and is modest in its claims. Yet over the past few decades, the evidence of global climate change and the emerging scientific consensus about the human impact on this process have led many governments to reach the conclusion that they need to invest time, money, and political will to address the problem through collective international action.

The bishops further urge that "Responses to global climate change should reflect our interdependence and common responsibility for the future of our planet" and point out that "climate change poses the question 'What does our generation owe to generations yet unborn?'"[19]

Fourteen years later, the situation was hardly any better, as we read from Pope Francis in *Laudato Si'*:

> The climate is a common good, belonging to all and meant for all. . . . A very solid scientific consensus indicates that we are presently witnessing a disturbing warming of the climatic system. . . . Humanity is called to recognize the need for changes of lifestyle, production and consumption, in order to combat this warming or at least the human causes which produce or aggravate it. It is true that there are other factors, . . . yet a number of scientific studies indicate that most global warming in recent decades is due to the great concentration of greenhouse gases (carbon dioxide, methane, nitrogen oxides and others) released mainly as a result of human activity.[20]

"Changes of lifestyle"—a daunting prospect, doubtlessly, but does that mean that we should throw up our collective hands in surrender? Is there nothing that we can do in response? Such changes involve sacrifice for the sake of others, in particular for those yet to be born. The Old Testament evidences a care and concern for generations yet to come. In Psalm 102, for example, God's glory and goodness are to be written down for the sake of future generations: "Let this be recorded for a generation to come, / so that a people yet unborn may praise the Lord" (Psalm 102:18). Sirach also sees the need to pass down teaching for the sake of the future: "I will again pour out teaching like prophecy, / and leave it to all future generations" (24:33).

In the New Testament, Jesus' sacrificial death is seen as a model for disciples of all times to follow, as in 1 John 3:16: "We know love by this, that he laid down his life for us—and we ought to lay down our lives for one another." We also have a beautiful teaching on self-sacrifice in Galatians 5:13: "For you were called to freedom, brothers and sisters; only do not use your freedom as an opportunity for self-indulgence, but through love become slaves to one another." It is clear that the Bible sees us as having responsibility for others, including those who will come after us. I wonder if we should consider making the stretch to conclude that we sin if we turn our backs on future generations and do damage to their collective patrimony without at least pausing to reflect on the consequences of our actions.

What, indeed, are the consequences if we do nothing whatsoever? What if we give in to denial, pretend that no problems exist, and leave things as they stand? In *Laudate Deum*, Pope Francis comments on the passage of time since he wrote *Laudato Si'* and reflects:

> I have realized that our responses have not been adequate, while the world in which we live is collapsing and may be nearing the breaking point. In

Chapter Four

>addition to this possibility, it is indubitable that the impact of climate change will increasingly prejudice the lives and families of many persons. We will feel its effects in the areas of healthcare, sources of employment, access to resources, housing, forced migrations, etc.[21]

In June of 2022, an article appeared in the New York Times that might give some pause for thought. The article is entitled "As the Great Salt Lake Dries Up, Utah Faces An 'Environmental Nuclear Bomb'" and presents a sobering perspective about just one place on our planet facing the detrimental effects of climate change. As the article explains, the Great Salt Lake in Utah has already shrunk by two thirds, and if this trend continues, beyond a number of other ecological problems, there is a serious danger that arsenic, high levels of which are in the bed of the lake, could be occasionally borne by wind storms to the lungs of residents around the Great Salt Lake, effectively three fourths of the population of Utah. As the article points out, saving the lake would require allowing more snow in the mountains to melt down into the lake, but this involves a changed availability of water for both residents and farmers, which poses its own problems.[22] Whatever may come of it, situations of the sort seem likely to become more common if we do not work together—if we do not "hold hands and shoot for the stars." Naïve? Maybe, but can we afford not to try?

For Reflection:

- What is your opinion regarding climate change? Do you believe that it is a problem exacerbated by human activity or do you see it more as normal cyclical changes in the general course of our planetary history? What scientific data do you know that would support your view?

- What kind of sacrifices would you be willing to make for the sake of the future of the planet? Do you deem these sacrifices to be part of your faith commitment?

Chapter Five

A Planetary Challenge: Going Green for the Blue Planet

In the last chapter, we reflected on the idea of sacrifice for the sake of the future. Considering the sacrifices that some people are capable of making for the sake of others can be very inspirational. My undergraduate degree is in history, and I have long been a student of the American Civil War. My particular love for the hallowed ground of Gettysburg stems from my first trip there when my parents brought my siblings and me to tour the battlefield for my thirteenth birthday. Over the years, I have been back more times than I can count. Of all the monuments one finds there, one of the most impressive to me is the monument of a Union soldier charging forward that is dedicated to the First Minnesota Regiment. Theirs is a story of tremendous self-sacrifice for a cause greater than themselves.

On the second day of the battle, two entire brigades of Confederate soldiers had overrun Union forces, charging through the Peach Orchard and fast approaching the Union line at Cemetery Ridge. Union General Winfield Scott Hancock saw that only 262 men of the First Minnesota Regiment were on hand to stop them. He ordered them forward; their charge into a force numbering around 1,500 was so fierce that even though it lasted only a few minutes, it held the Confederates up just long enough for General Hancock to bring up reinforcements. This helped to save the center of the Union line. Of the 262 men who made the charge, however, only 47 returned from the field, a casualty rate of more than 82 percent, the highest of any Union regiment for the entire war.

Such heroism and courage make any paltry "sacrifice" that I might perform seem extremely lame in comparison. At the same time, reflecting on the sacrifices of others can hopefully inspire me to be just a little better and to want to give of myself in whatever small way I might be able to for the sake of others. In our Christian heritage, what can be more inspiring or can possibly compare to the self-sacrifice of Jesus on the cross for our sake? In Hebrews 9:26, we read: "But as it is, he has appeared once for all at the end of the age to remove sin by the sacrifice of himself." In the book of the prophet Isaiah, there are four "songs" of the Suffering Servant which have taken on much significance in Judaism and particularly in Christianity. While the earlier chapters of Isaiah present us with a vision of a kingly messiah, it is clear to me that Jesus saw himself more along the lines of the servant suffering for the sake of others in those latter chapters, as in Isaiah 53:5: "But he was wounded for our transgressions, / crushed for our iniquities; / upon him was the punishment that made us whole, / and by his bruises we are healed."

The idea of "going green for the blue planet" necessarily entails at least a small level of sacrifice, some willingness

Chapter Five

on my part to be "inconvenienced" in some way. When my parents' neighborhood first began recycling efforts quite a number of years back, it struck me as both strange and bothersome. I was used to simply tossing everything into the garbage. All of a sudden, I found myself collecting things in separate bags for my parents and putting the bags out at curbside on specific days according to the schedule set by the mayor's office. It seemed an inconvenience at the time, but now it has become so normal to me that I don't even think about it anymore. It has become so ordinary, in fact, that, as mentioned in chapter 3, when I have found myself somewhere that does not have such a recycling system in place, I find myself instinctively feeling that something is not as it should be.

The willingness to allow myself to be inconvenienced, in whatever small way, involves a willingness to undergo some level of conversion to change my focus from my own issues to the needs and benefits of others. What this essentially means is that we need a change of attitude and/or behavior. In our biblical tradition, we have many different examples of people undergoing a conversion, a profound turnabout. In the Old Testament, the book of Ruth is a magnificent story of a Moabite woman who, despite the strictures of Deuteronomy 23:3–6 against Moabites entering the community of Israel, says in those beautiful words to her mother-in-law Naomi, "Where you go, I will go; / where you lodge, I will lodge; / your people shall be my people, / and your God my God" (Ruth 1:16). Not only does Ruth give up her Moabite religion to become a faithful believer in the God of Israel, but, as noted in the first chapter, she becomes the great-grandmother of King David.

One of the most dramatic stories of conversion in the Bible is so important that it is recounted three times in the Acts of the Apostles (chapters 9, 22, and 26) as well as (in less detail and in non-narrative fashion) in the Letter to the Galatians (chapter 2), namely, the conversion of Paul. Acts 9:1–18 tells the story of Paul (then Saul) on the road to Damascus, overcome by a light from heaven and thrown to the ground, where he hears a voice asking, "Saul, Saul, why do you persecute me?" (verse 4). The speaker identifies himself as Jesus when Paul asks who he is. Paul's process of conversion starts, then, with his persecution of the early Christian community and leads to him becoming the greatest missionary in Christian history. The import of Paul's conversion for that very Christian history is, in fact, impossible to overestimate, as he is the one who really brings Christianity out into the wider world from its Judean and Galilean matrix.

Stories such as these are a bit more dramatic, but a conversion can be simpler and even of a somewhat unique nature. Pope Francis writes of one such situation in a section of *Laudato Si'* entitled "Ecological Conversion," where we read:

> This conversion calls for a number of attitudes which together foster a spirit of generous care, full of tenderness. First, it entails gratitude and gratuitousness, a recognition that the world is God's loving gift, and that we are called quietly

> to imitate his generosity in self-sacrifice and good works: "Do not let your left hand know what your right hand is doing . . . and your Father who sees in secret will reward you" (*Mt* 6:3–4). It also entails a loving awareness that we are not disconnected from the rest of creatures, but joined in a splendid universal communion. . . . By developing our individual, God-given capacities, an ecological conversion can inspire us to greater creativity and enthusiasm in resolving the world's problems and in offering ourselves to God "as a living sacrifice, holy and acceptable" (*Rom* 12:1). We do not understand our superiority as a reason for personal glory or irresponsible dominion, but rather as a different capacity which, in its turn, entails a serious responsibility stemming from our faith.[23]

An interesting concept, but how can I make it play out practically in my own life? How do I show the benefits of such a conversion in my own reality? And how does a conversion of this kind impact the lives of those around me and the world as a whole? Pope Francis's strongly biblical vision of the need for proactive engagement to save our "common home," planet earth, is a clarion call to all of us to act responsibly.

Conversion best occurs when one recognizes the need for change and then acts accordingly. If we can but remind ourselves that the world is God's and is, in God's opinion "very good" (Genesis 1:31), then we can ask ourselves if we have given it the respect and reverence that it deserves. If our answer is "no," then hopefully we can find ourselves motivated to make a change. What can drive us to do so? One way is to keep in mind and heart what we are told in Wisdom 11:24—12:1:

> For you love all things that exist, / and detest none of the things that you have made, / for you would not have made anything if you had hated it. / How would anything have endured if you had not willed it? / Or how would anything not called forth by you have been preserved? / You spare all things, for they are yours, O Lord, you who love the living. / For your immortal spirit is in all things.

As Pope Francis reminds us in *Laudate Deum*: "The Bible tells us: 'God saw everything that he had made, and indeed, it was very good' (*Gen* 1:31). His is 'the earth with all that is in it' (*Deut* 10:14). For this reason, he tells us that, 'the land shall not be sold in perpetuity, for the land is mine; with me you are but aliens and tenants' (*Lev* 25:23)."[24]

Chapter 3 looked at the serious problem of pollution and the amount of damage that we, as a human species, have done from time immemorial, and continue to do to this beautiful earth of ours. Chapter 4 reflected on climate change denial as a species of "defense mechanism" because of the sheer scale of the problem. But is such denial responsible?

Psalm 11 gives us some food for thought as the psalm begins with a sense of frustration and a temptation to give up in the face of a difficult challenge: "In the LORD I take refuge; how can you say to me, / 'Flee like a bird to the mountains; / for look, the wicked bend the bow, / they have fitted their arrow to the string, / to shoot in the dark at the upright in heart. / If the foundations are destroyed, / what can the righteous do?'" (verses 1–3). The psalmist, effectively, ponders advice to "turn and run" in the face of a threat that seems to be more than he can handle. The easy route would be, of course, to avoid the problem. Instead, in the fourth verse he remembers God's presence in the Temple and the assurance that, from heaven, God does not lose sight of anything that is done here on the earth, whether by the righteous or the unrighteous. The psalm then concludes: "For the LORD is righteous; / he loves righteous deeds; / the upright shall behold his face" (verse 7). In essence, the psalm reminds me to not lose hope, to not give up even when a situation appears totally beyond my control—because I am not, ultimately the one in control anyway.

In the Acts of the Apostles, after Peter's speech at Pentecost—in which he proclaims Jesus crucified and risen and declares that "God has made him both Lord and Messiah, this Jesus whom you crucified" (Acts 2:36)—the crowd is shaken and needs a little direction: "Now when they heard this, they were cut to the heart and said to Peter and to the other apostles, 'Brothers, what should we do?'" (2:37). In the face of the enormous challenge that confronts us in trying to deal with the problematic situation of the environment, I would certainly appreciate a little guidance too. "What should we do?" is a question that makes much sense to me. It indicates a desire to *do* something, to act on the knowledge I now have.

I can imagine a variety of possible responses. I could decide to give up my present activity and devote all of my time and energy to environmental concerns and challenges—that's one end of the spectrum of responses. On the other end, I could simply throw up my hands, admit that all of my best efforts will only go so far without commitment from everyone else together, and basically "call it a day." The tactic that I prefer personally is somewhere in the middle: to act in whatever ways I can in order to make things just a little bit better and to trust that others will do the same in their own small ways, and be confident that, when added up, it will, in fact, make a difference for the better.

So, what should we do? We probably don't have to go far from home to discover ways to make a difference. Contacting one's local municipality is a start. Even closer to home, there might be initiatives coming from one's parish or other faith communities in the area. In such cases, we can join with others to make a difference. Working with others can help reinforce the idea that there are many who are committed to making things better, plus we are more likely to be able to see the effects of our efforts. I remember a number of years ago seeing how some relatives of mine in the Chicago area pitched in with their neighbors to clean up a local park and were even able to set aside a community garden for people to grow vegetables and the like.

Chapter Five

More personally, a simple internet search can find a number of easy, practical suggestions for day-to-day life that can make a difference while not being overly burdensome. In 2020 the British newspaper The Guardian published an excellent article entitled "50 Simple Ways to Make Your Life Greener."[25] In it, the authors focused on various dynamics of life and presented suggestions even for different sections of one's household: the kitchen, the home in general, the garden, clothing (both new and old), the bathroom, and finally, general ideas regarding the planet as a whole. While I would be skeptical that many people—however "simple" the ways—would put all fifty of these suggestions into practice, many of the ideas really are so simple that it would not be a terrible inconvenience to make a handful a reality. It strikes me that one could also have the side benefit of saving a great deal of money annually by (just for example) making the most of leftovers in meal planning; keeping the house free of drafts, especially during the colder weather; and learning how to mend older clothing.

For those who prefer fewer items to have to remember, Consumer Reports offers "10 Quick Tips for Going Green at Home."[26] Almost all of the suggestions are very practical ideas such as (again) sealing air leaks and unplugging electronic devices that continue to drain electricity even when powered down. In both cases (again), this would not only be beneficial to the planet, but would also have the concrete benefit of putting money back into people's pockets. Maybe that is not the most altruistic of motives, but why not reap another personal benefit while doing something positive for the world or, minimally, for our own local environment?

After some of my comments in earlier chapters, it may seem strange to be emphasizing a host of simpler ideas in the present context. I do not want to walk back any of those thoughts and reflections. But the point to be made here is simply that while the situation in our world is admittedly grave and requires a much more sustained commitment to be responsible stewards of God's creation, as mentioned in chapter 1, "going green for the blue planet" need not be overly painful or stress-filled if we simply attempt to do our part. Much needs to be done on a wider scale, and a willingness to contact our elected representatives to make our opinions known, for example, can go a long way in that regard. But from our own standpoints, we can find ways to make a difference starting locally and branching out from there. I cannot change the world, but I can change my own little piece of it.

For Reflection:

- Are there any green initiatives in your parish, diocese, neighborhood, or town in which you can take part?
- What practices can you take up in your own life that would positively affect either the environment in general or at least in your local area?

Chapter Six

Lessons from a Pandemic

A number of years back, I spent a delightful day with a very dear friend of mine and his wife in southern Italy. After a delicious and relaxing *pranzo* (lunch) at their home in Bagnoli, we took a nice long walk. The town in which they live is very close to Naples, the city from which my family originates. It is right on the shore, so we walked out onto an enormous pier jutting out well into the bay that afforded an absolutely magnificent view of the Gulf of Pozzuoli. They explained to me that the town had been known for steel production and that the pier was used to load steel onto ships until the plant was closed around thirty years ago. The area had been, as one can imagine given the factory, terribly polluted, but the water actually looked clean from my point of view. In fact, we saw numerous people swimming, and I commented on that to my friends. My friends explained that while the water has become much cleaner over the years, it is still not really safe to swim there and that the people we saw doing so were actually putting themselves at some risk.

Given my comments in chapter 3 about my friend who developed cellulitis in Lake Erie, I would worry about those Italians whom I saw swimming near Naples. I certainly wouldn't even consider it myself, but the thing that struck me even at the time was how, effectively, the sea was in the slow process of reclaiming itself (as was true of Lake Erie). It seemed to me, given enough years without adding more pollutants ("ay, there's the rub," again), the bay would return to a more natural and cleaner state of affairs. This incident came back to my memory more than once, particularly during the COVID-19 lockdown. At that time, there were so many stories from all around the world about how various cities absolutely plagued by smog and air pollution were suddenly experiencing the "strange" phenomenon of relatively clean air due to the lack of motor vehicles on the roads. The contrast visible in photos comparing the pre-pandemic hazy, polluted skies with the clear blue skies during lockdown was remarkable and even somewhat eerie. Even more dramatic was the visible presence of more and more wildlife in cities where the absence of human activity, cars, and so on made them more attractive to birds and animals. This is, I would suggest, at least one positive lesson that we can learn from the decidedly negative experience of pandemic lockdown, an experience that almost seems surreal to recall whenever I think about it.

What is "Normal"?

A 2021 BBC News article entitled "Then and Now: Pandemic Clears the Air" noted the dramatic improvement of air quality during the COVID-19 lockdown but also that the air returned quickly to "normal" as soon as

Chapter Six

the lockdowns were lifted.[27] This latter sense of "normal," unfortunately, serves as a hard lesson to learn from the pandemic, namely, that while we can do better, we can just as quickly fall back into a negative trend. Thinking back to my time in Bagnoli and the phenomenon of clear air quality during the lockdown makes me wonder about the power of the earth to heal itself. I suggest that it is a good idea for us to ask ourselves if there is anything that we can do to aid that process.

In August of 2019, prior to the pandemic and any lockdowns, the United Nations Environment Program posted an article entitled "Nature Can Still Heal Itself, If We Give It the Urgent Attention It Needs." The article notes that there is a healing power of nature and that "nature-based solutions, which feature a holistic approach to land use by leveraging the existing resources nature has in stock, enable us to make use of the planet's intrinsic restorative capacity." The article points out how both society-wide and individual action is necessary to potentially "scale back at least part of the unfolding disaster."[28]

In *Laudato Si'*, the encyclical letter we have already invoked throughout the course of these chapters, Pope Francis generally takes a more proactive stance than fits the theme and dynamics of this particular chapter. Nonetheless, in a section entitled "Politics and Economy in Dialogue for Human Fulfilment," we read:

> Where profits alone count, there can be no thinking about the rhythms of nature, its phases of decay

and regeneration, or the complexity of ecosystems which may be gravely upset by human intervention. Moreover, biodiversity is considered at most a deposit of economic resources available for exploitation, with no serious thought for the real value of things, their significance for persons and cultures, or the concerns and needs of the poor.[29]

The ideas of "rhythms of nature" and "phases of decay and regeneration" without human intervention make me wonder about the capacity of nature to fall back into those rhythms if we but give it a chance and allow for the possibility of regeneration to take place.

An Old Testament Perspective

In the Old Testament, there is a concept involving agriculture that I noted in chapter 4. This practice always seems strange enough to my students when I first mention it, namely, the tradition of the Sabbath Year. But this confusion increases when we move on to the tradition of the so-called Jubilee Year. However, in our present context, both ideas might be curiously instructive as regards the idea of nature having a capacity to heal itself. According to Leviticus chapter 25, concerning the Sabbath Year:

> The LORD spoke to Moses on Mount Sinai, saying: Speak to the people of Israel and say to them: When you enter the land that I am giving you, the land shall observe a sabbath for the LORD. Six

Chapter Six

> years you shall sow your field, and six years you shall prune your vineyard, and gather in their yield; but in the seventh year there shall be a sabbath of complete rest for the land, a sabbath for the LORD: you shall not sow your field or prune your vineyard. You shall not reap the aftergrowth of your harvest or gather the grapes of your unpruned vine: it shall be a year of complete rest for the land. You may eat what the land yields during its sabbath—you, your male and female slaves, your hired and your bound laborers who live with you; for your livestock also, and for the wild animals in your land all its yield shall be for food. (Leviticus 25:1–7)

In Exodus 23:10–11, we see that the reason for this practice is primarily care for the poor: "For six years you shall sow your land and gather in its yield; but the seventh year you shall let it rest and lie fallow, so that the poor of your people may eat; and what they leave the wild animals may eat. You shall do the same with your vineyard, and with your olive orchard." The rationale of these two passages is not practical, however, but primarily theological. In the Exodus passage, while not necessarily given a directly theological meaning, it can be seen as such by its compassionate nature deriving from the compassion of God to care for the oppressed and the vulnerable. In the Leviticus account, it is more clearly theological, invoking Sabbath rest: just as God rested after Creation in Genesis, so must the Israelites rest on the day of the Sabbath. And in this context, even the land will get its Sabbath rest!

Where things begin to get more confusing for my students is what follows this section in Leviticus. Starting with verse 8, Leviticus describes what is known as the Jubilee Year, when, at the end of forty-nine years, a fiftieth year begins with the blowing of the ram's horn, the *shofar*, on the Day of Atonement (Yom Kippur, the traditional Jewish feast of repentance and reconciliation). This year involves the return of land to families who had been forced to sell it because of impoverishment and the liberation of Israelites from debt slavery. But for our purposes here and now, it is another year in which the land must be left fallow. What this means, therefore, is that the land remains unworked for not one, but for two years straight in the forty-ninth and fiftieth years.

How, students have asked me, is that possible? The text itself gives an answer which puts everything into theological perspective:

> The land will yield its fruit, and you will eat your fill and live on it securely. Should you ask, "What shall we eat in the seventh year, if we may not sow or gather in our crop?" I will order my blessing for you in the sixth year, so that it will yield a crop for three years. When you sow in the eighth year, you will be eating from the old crop; until the ninth year, when its produce comes in, you shall eat the old. (Leviticus 25:19–22)

So, we have the land left fallow every seventh year and then, following the forty-ninth year (a Sabbath Year), likewise in

Chapter Six

the fiftieth. The Jubilee Year becomes especially important over time for its emphasis on liberation and restoration.

The Jesus Tradition

In Luke 4:18–19, Jesus makes powerful use of Isaiah 61:1–2a, which emphasizes the liberation aspect of the Jubilee Year. His purpose is to set forth the very program for his mission in the Gospel when he proclaims in the synagogue of Nazareth: "The Spirit of the Lord is upon me, / because he has anointed me / to bring good news to the poor. / He has sent me to proclaim release to the captives / and recovery of sight to the blind, / to let the oppressed go free, / to proclaim the year of the Lord's favor." It is clear that the Jubilee Year was an important concept in the Torah and in the prophets, and then reflected in the New Testament.

Looking at the land, is there really anything to the idea of giving it a Sabbath and/or then a jubilee rest? As a matter of fact, it might be surprising—particularly for those of us with little or no knowledge of agriculture—to hear that the answer is yes. There are actually very good agricultural reasons for such a practice. In an article entitled "What Is Fallow Ground: Are There Any Benefits of Fallowing Soil," we read that fallowing the land has been a means of sustainable land management for centuries in many parts of the world (the author notes the Mediterranean, North Africa, and Asia, in particular). Nutrients can be replenished and, the article asserts, "fallowing the soil can cause potassium and phosphorus from deep below to rise toward the soil surface where it can be used by crops later." Fallowing soil also "raises levels of carbon, nitrogen and organic matter, improves moisture holding capacity, and increases beneficial microorganisms in the soil."[30] All of this seems to shore up the idea that nature has an amazing ability to restore itself if just given the chance, as we accidentally learned from the pandemic lockdown.

Fallowing the soil is merely one key way in which human beings have learned to, effectively, "work with" nature. As *Laudate Deum* notes:

> For this reason, a healthy ecology is also the result of interaction between human beings and the environment, as occurs in the indigenous cultures and has occurred for centuries in different regions of the earth. Human groupings have often "created" an environment, reshaping it in some way without destroying it or endangering it. The great present-day problem is that the technocratic paradigm has destroyed that healthy and harmonious relationship. In any event, the indispensable need to move beyond that paradigm, so damaging and destructive, will not be found in a denial of the human being, but include the interaction of natural systems "with social systems."[31]

Reestablishing a "healthy and harmonious relationship" can serve to allow us to work with nature in such a way as to avoid unduly harming it, and by allowing it to heal itself from what changes we have wrought.

Chapter Six

Even though Jesus was not a farmer (he is called "the carpenter" in Mark 6:3 and "the carpenter's son" in Matthew 13:55), he had a good knowledge of the workings and rhythms of nature and of the agricultural milieu, as his parables demonstrate. He was, after all, from rural Galilee. He speaks of fig trees, mustard seeds, flowers of the field, the wheat and the weeds, animals such as sheep and birds, and the seed and the earth. This last, as in the Parable of the Sower (Mark chapter 4 and parallels) is one of the few parables that Jesus ever explains to his disciples in the Gospels. Each of the aforementioned images would have spoken easily and quite familiarly to his audience.

That is not the case for so many of us today who live in urban and suburban areas. In an article appearing in the *American Baptist Quarterly* entitled "'A Sower Went Out to Sow': An Agrarian Reading of the New Testament," the author notes how good soil (topsoil) is cared for, and that a knowledge of care for the soil can enrich our view of Jesus' Parable of the Sower. He tells us that, in contrast to a more "industrial" view of the parable, effectively cut off from knowledge of how agriculture works, "An agrarian reading of the parable implies that those with ears to hear should so tend the soil of their lives, their communities, and their congregations in such a way that the Word of the kingdom might find a fruitful resting place."[32] Jesus' original audience would have had a better sense of this meaning than we do, given that their very survival depended upon the soil. Overworking or exhausting the soil does not give it the chance to replenish itself; fallowing the soil was a key means of care of which the ancients were well aware and which demonstrates, as we learned the hard way during the course of the COVID-19 lockdown, that the earth has an uncanny ability to renew and rejuvenate itself.

Learning from the Need for Rest

The concept of the Sabbath and Jubilee Years are literally enshrined in this biblical teaching. While they serve the practical purpose of allowing the land to do what it can to heal itself and to make itself more productive, as the aforementioned article "What is Fallow Ground," demonstrates, it is important to note that this is not the primary reason these years are commemorated. Both the Sabbath and Jubilee Years are fundamentally theological. The emphasis upon care for the poor in the Sabbath Year (as in Exodus chapter 23) is part and parcel of the compassionate nature of the Law rooted in the compassion of God. God liberates the enslaved Israelites in the Exodus and cares for them in the wilderness. This is an attitude that is to be imitated in their interactions with others. In Leviticus, the demand that the land receive its Sabbaths is rooted in the Sabbath rest of God in Genesis. The Jubilee is rooted in the belief that the land ultimately belongs to God. It is not to be bought and sold permanently. Rather, it belongs to the Lord who then presents it to Israel as tenants, from which point it is parceled out to the tribes and then to families in each tribe; and it was to remain in their families.

This latter sense of responsibility for the land is powerfully reflected in the account of Naboth's vineyard in 1

Chapter Six

Kings. King Ahab says to Naboth, "Give me your vineyard, so that I may have it for a vegetable garden, because it is near my house; I will give you a better vineyard for it; or, if it seems good to you, I will give you its value in money." Naboth refuses, saying, "The Lord forbid that I should give you my ancestral inheritance" (1 Kings 21:2, 3). We can see through all of this that Israel was entrusted by God with the stewardship of God's own land. Ahab later connived, through the machinations of his evil wife Jezebel, to confiscate Naboth's vineyard, confirming that he did not understand God's plan for the land and his people (see 1 Kings chapter 21).

Living through the COVID-19 pandemic was difficult, to say the least. For those of us who were caring for elderly or sick parents at the time, it was particularly frightening. It is hard to look back and think of anything positive from what we experienced, but at least it did teach us some key lessons regarding the care of our planet. First, in an overarching way, we were reminded that nature has a remarkable ability to restore itself. Second (and connected to the first), the phenomenon of relatively cleaner air in ordinarily polluted cities showed us that we actually do have the ability to facilitate that process by changing our habits. The many cities suddenly seeing cleaner air due to fewer emissions from cars, buses, trucks, and other vehicles showed us that nature can begin to heal itself if we succeed in finding a way to reduce and/or eliminate damaging fossil fuel emissions. But third, we learned that we can easily undermine any progress that we make. We learned that going back to our old ways of doing things would return us just as quickly to living once more with smog and pollution.

For Reflection:

- Is there anything that you can do, such as taking public transportation, carpooling, walking, or biking, rather than driving that might help to reduce the emission of pollutants?

- Do you really believe that the land (as well as the sea and the air) ultimately belongs to God?

Chapter Seven

Stewards of Creation

When I was in college, a drummer friend of mine was going away for a vacation. I don't know why, but he was nice enough to offer to loan me his drum kit for a couple of weeks while, just by chance, my parents (fortunately for them) were also away. I am a guitarist and bassist, not a drummer, but for two weeks, I had an absolute blast trying (unsuccessfully) to develop some semblance of a drum technique. My friend was letting me keep an eye on his prized possession, his drum kit. He was fine with me playing them as much as I wanted. I could practice and use them at will, but there were certain limits. It wasn't my prerogative to have other friends over for a jam session and let them use his drums. I could pound away to my heart's content, but not to the point of breaking through the drum heads. And, while doing my best to imitate great classic rock drummers, I certainly could not try the ultimate rocker imitation of kicking them in when I was done playing. My job was to be a steward of his valued belongings. I needed to keep in mind that what I used did not belong to me and that I was being trusted to keep them in good shape for their actual owner.

The Meaning of Stewardship

What is a steward? According to the dictionary, a steward is:

1. one employed in a large household or estate to manage domestic concerns (such as the supervision of servants, collection of rents, and keeping of accounts)

2. shop steward

3. a fiscal agent

4a. an employee on a ship, airplane, bus, or train who manages the provisioning of food and attends passengers,

b. one appointed to supervise the provision and distribution of food and drink in an institution

5. one who actively directs affairs: manager[33]

We can see that to be a steward is to hold a position of trust and of significant responsibility. A truly effective steward is aware that he or she is both caring for the goods of others and being trusted to manage that property well.

There is an interesting Old Testament passage in which we see God removing one steward in favor of another who will do a better job. In the book of Isaiah, the prophet is sent to "this steward, to Shebna," a servant of king Hezekiah, with a rather harsh message: "The LORD is about to hurl you away violently, my fellow. He will seize firm hold on you, whirl you round and round, and throw you like a ball into a wide land; there you shall die, and there your splendid chariots shall lie, O you disgrace to your master's house!" (Isaiah 22:17–18). The implication seems to be that Shebna has misused his high office for his own glorification rather than being concerned, as steward of the king, with his actual responsibilities. What angers the Lord is that Shebna has cut out a tomb for himself on a high place where he has no family members buried (see verse 16), so it would seem to be a memorial to himself where he does not have the right to be; the reference to his "splendid chariots" also indicates using resources for his own purposes rather than his master's.

Shebna is told that the Lord will then call someone who will properly perform his functions as steward: Eliakim, the son of Hilkiah. The Lord will

> clothe him with your robe and bind your sash on him. I will commit your authority to his hand, and he shall be a father to the inhabitants of Jerusalem and to the house of Judah. I will place on his shoulder the key of the house of David; he shall open, and no one shall shut; he shall shut, and no one shall open. I will fasten him like a peg in a secure place, and he will become a throne of honor to his ancestral house. And they will hang on him the whole weight of his ancestral house, the offspring and issue, every small vessel, from the cups to all the flagons. (Isaiah 22:21–24)

In this passage, it is clear that stewardship is not to be taken lightly; when a steward of the kingdom is not carrying out his duties faithfully, he is replaced by God himself with one who will exercise his stewardship in a trustworthy manner.

In *Laudato Si'*, Pope Francis notes that:

> An inadequate presentation of Christian anthropology gave rise to a wrong understanding of the relationship between human beings and the world. Often, what was handed on was a Promethean vision of mastery over the world, which gave the impression that the protection of nature was something that only the faint-hearted cared about. Instead, our "dominion" over the universe should be understood more properly in the sense of responsible stewardship.[34]

This "Promethean vision" refers to what I noted at the beginning of this book about a misunderstanding of the terms "have dominion" and "subdue" that appear in the Genesis accounts of Creation. Throughout the book, we have reflected on the idea of the call to be the stewards of God's creation as a corrective thereof.

The term *steward* appears a number of times in the New Testament as the translation of a particular Greek word *oikonomos*. It is not always translated as "steward" in the New Revised Standard Version of the Bible, but there are some very telling passages in which it is used precisely as such. There is a section in First Corinthians in which Paul is trying to change the Corinthian Christian community's way of thinking about apostolic ministry. He writes: "Think of us in this way, as servants of Christ and stewards of God's mysteries" (4:1). It is in the immediately following verse that he tells us something particularly important concerning the character and work of a steward: "Moreover, it is required of stewards that they be found trustworthy." The steward is not the owner, but one who has been entrusted by the owner to care for the owner's property or, in this case, mission. In the Letter to Titus, in discussing the qualities of a bishop, we read: "For a bishop, as God's steward, must be blameless;. . . he must be hospitable, a lover of goodness, prudent, upright, devout, and self-controlled" (1:7–8). In describing how Christians are to behave toward each other, the author of First Peter writes: "Like good stewards of the manifold grace of God, serve one another with whatever gift each of you has received" (4:10). This advice is a reminder that literally all that we have does not truly belong to us, but rather is ours only because it was given to us first by God for us to use in trustworthy service to and for others.

Jesus himself shows a concern for good and responsible stewardship. One particularly powerful passage in which this is evident uses the Greek word *oikonomos* (NRSV "manager"; NABRE "steward"). The passage reads:

> And the Lord said, "Who then is the faithful and prudent manager [literally, "steward"] whom his master will put in charge of his slaves, to give them their allowance of food at the proper time? Blessed is that slave whom his master will find at work when he arrives. Truly I tell you, he will put that one in charge of all his possessions." (Luke 12:42–44)

The responsible steward is rewarded for his work.

Whose World Is This?

So, do we believe that we "own" the world, that it is ours to do with as we choose? If that is the case, then we can feel free to use up all of its resources, to wipe out its forests (thus affecting the oxygen content of the air), to render its soil unusable, to turn its waters virtually undrinkable. We may need to live with the results, but if we believe that this is our exclusive belonging, then we can try to defend our negative actions as doing with our own possession as we decide. After all, in the Parable of the Laborers in the Vineyard, doesn't the owner say, "Am I not allowed to do what I choose with what belongs to me?" (Of course, that is taking the entire passage out of context, as the owner's next words are "Or are you envious because I am generous?" [Matthew 20:15]). But can the attitude of thinking that we can do as we please with what we see as ours be justified by the Scriptures? I strongly suggest that the Bible would answer that question with an emphatic and resounding "No."

Psalm 95 puts things into a nice perspective for us, letting us know in no uncertain terms to whom the whole of creation belongs.

> O come, let us sing to the LORD; / let us make a joyful noise to the rock of our salvation! / Let us come into his presence with thanksgiving; / let us make a joyful noise to him with songs of praise! / For the LORD is a great God, / and a great King above all gods. / In his hand are the depths of the earth; / the heights of the mountains are his also.

Chapter Seven

> / The sea is his, for he made it, / and the dry land, which his hands have formed. / O come, let us worship and bow down, / let us kneel before the Lord, our Maker! / For he is our God, / and we are the people of his pasture, / and the sheep of his hand. (Psalm 95:1–7)

The psalmist makes it crystal clear: The world belongs to God and not to us.

The author of Sirach also reflects on the wondrous beauty of the cosmos: "I will now call to mind the works of the Lord, / and will declare what I have seen. / By the word of the Lord his works are made; / and all his creatures do his will. / The sun looks down on everything with its light, / and the work of the Lord is / full of his glory" (Sirach 42:15–16). Again, the biblical text reminds us that creation is the work of God rather than something haphazard or the result of any effort of our own. Psalm 19:1 shows creation attesting to God's glory: "The heavens are telling the glory of God; / and the firmament proclaims his handiwork." We should also recall the beautiful passage from Wisdom cited in chapter 2, about the wholesomeness of "the generative forces of the world" and the absence of the dominion of Hades on this earth (1:14).

In the midst of all this wonder, it might be nice to recognize that we are placed on this earth by God, the world which John 3:16 tells us that "God so loved," as a particularly blessed piece of God's wondrous creation. Jesus speaks of our intrinsic value in God's eyes over and against what he puts forth as examples of the beauty of what God has created and how God cares for other created beings. In the Gospel of Luke, for example, Jesus begins by commenting that "Are not five sparrows sold for two pennies? Yet not one of them is forgotten in God's sight." He goes on to emphasize that each human being is "of more value than many sparrows" and exhorts us not to be afraid (Luke 12:6, 7). In the Gospel of Matthew, in teaching his disciples not to be worried, Jesus says: "And why do you worry about clothing? Consider the lilies of the field, how they grow; they neither toil nor spin, yet I tell you, even Solomon in all his glory was not clothed like one of these. But if God so clothes the grass of the field, which is alive today and tomorrow is thrown into the oven, will he not much more clothe you—you of little faith?" (Matthew 6:28–30).

Another key text that recognizes to whom this world really belongs is Psalm 50. In it, the psalmist quotes God, who "calls to the heavens above / and to the earth" (verse 4):

> Not for your sacrifices do I rebuke you; / your burnt offerings are continually before me. / I will not accept a bull from your house, / or goats from your folds. / For every wild animal of the forest is mine, / the cattle on a thousand hills. / I know all the birds of the air, / and all that moves in the field is mine. / If I were hungry, I would not tell you, / for the world and all that is in it is mine. / Do I eat the flesh of bulls, / or drink the blood of goats? / Offer to God a sacrifice of thanksgiving, / and pay your vows to the Most High. (verses 8–14)

Chapter Seven

The idea that "every wild animal of the forest" belongs to God is also powerfully borne out in the book of Job when God appears to answer Job's challenges. In the Divine Speeches, which extend from Job 38:1 through 41:34, the focus is both on cosmology and God's care for the animals, but more specifically the wild animals that are out of human control.

Of the animals listed, there is really only one that could actually be domesticated, namely the horse, and even that description puts the animal beyond normal human control:

> Do you give the horse its might? / Do you clothe its neck with mane? / Do you make it leap like the locust? / Its majestic snorting is terrible. / It paws violently, exults mightily; / it goes out to meet the weapons. / It laughs at fear, and is not dismayed; / it does not turn back from the sword. / . . . When the trumpet sounds, it says "Aha!" / From a distance it smells the battle, / the thunder of the captains, and the shouting. (Job 39:19–22, 25)

The type of horse that God describes is clearly not a plow horse or a normal horse for riding, but more precisely the war horse, which was, in warfare of centuries past, a very fearsome creature used by its rider effectively as a sort of additional weapon against those they would try to ride down or over. So even in this case, it is an animal beyond simple human control of which God is shown to be the Creator and preeminent caretaker. Again, the point is clear. The world is not ours, but God's. We are, nonetheless, placed here by God as a privileged part of that world, challenged by—but ultimately honored by—the command to "keep it" for its true owner and for those whom that owner has placed here with us.

Once More: Subdue, Have Dominion, or Safeguard?

As noted in chapter 1, Genesis 1:26-31, at the end of the first account of Creation, could be seen as a problematic text, given the commands to "have dominion" and to "subdue." I noted then how this can be taken in such a way as to justify doing whatever we wish with the world in which we live, but that it is then put into counterpoint with the second Creation account in Genesis 2:15 (as noted by Pope Francis in *Laudato Si'*), which tells how God placed the man in the garden "to till it and keep it." The Hebrew word *šmr* translated as "keep" has a range of meanings that includes ideas such as keep, watch, preserve, have charge of, guard, and protect. This, in my opinion, is where the concept of the human being as a steward of God's creation is best seen. The will of God as seen in Genesis 2:15 is that we make appropriate use of his creation ("till it"), but at the same time, that we safeguard it ("keep it"). What helps to keep us on track regarding this latter charge is if we remind ourselves that the world is not fundamentally our own, but God's, and that we are privileged to be placed here to enjoy it in all its magnificent beauty and not to mar it by our misuse of it.

If we can view ourselves as caring stewards of God's creation, we can start to change our attitude from one of subduing and dominating to one of protection and safeguarding for our collective use and for the use of those who will follow us. So, for example, when I make use of a plastic container for food, I can make certain that I will wash it out and put it in the recycling bin rather than simply toss it in the trash. If I live someplace where recycling efforts are not what they could or should be, I can try to do my part to work with others to change the situation and raise consciousness about the need to recycle items that otherwise would simply sit in a landfill and contribute to the poisoning of what belongs not to us, but to God.

A good steward should be wise enough to make use of the gifts and talents of those who can best help him or her with the responsible management of the goods under his or her care. If I can see myself as a steward of God's creation, can I work with others in order to accomplish the good that I simply cannot achieve on my own? Using the previous example of recycling efforts, my own voice can make a difference, but it can make a far bigger difference and be better heard if I have a whole chorus of voices singing along with me.

This uniting of voices is essential if any true progress on a wider level is ever to be realized. Our individual stewardship is vital, again, particularly with something as simple as recycling efforts, but what about enormous issues such as climate change? Maybe the only way to proceed in any effective manner is to draw out on a social dimension to stewardship, a social dimension that would then need to reach even the national and international levels. In *Laudate Deum*, Pope Francis addresses this idea:

I ask everyone to accompany this pilgrimage of reconciliation with the world that is our home and to help make it more beautiful, because that commitment has to do with our personal dignity and highest values. At the same time, I cannot deny that it is necessary to be honest and recognize that the most effective solutions will not come from individual efforts alone, but above all from major political decisions on the national and international level.[35]

The succeeding line begins "Nonetheless, every little bit helps,"[36] but the point just made is clear that much is beyond our individual control. The lessons of the Scriptures may challenge us to recognize the call to be stewards of God's creation individually, but we should also consider the call on a much larger scale as well, which is, maybe, the far more difficult task.

For Reflection:

- Genesis chapters 1 and 2 give us two different ideas concerning our use of creation, to subdue and have dominion or to keep. Which seems better to you and why?

- Thinking of yourself as a steward of God's creation, how do you see yourself best living up to the trust that God has placed in you? What concrete steps can you take to fulfill this vision?

Afterword

And so, we come to the end of *What Does the Bible Say About... Creation?* There were three reasons that made this a difficult book to write from the outset. First and foremost, I am not a scientist in general, nor a climatologist in particular. In that sense, much of what I reflected upon was, to put it mildly, a good way out of my academic area of expertise as a biblical scholar. I needed to read what people with expertise in the field were saying as well as—given the faith perspective of the book—reading the reflections of religious figures such as Pope Francis and the United States Conference of Catholic Bishops to help spark my own thoughts on the topic. Second, as noted in the introduction, there was quite a bit of guesswork involved as to what the biblical authors would think about the environmental issues facing us today, since they would not have been able to even imagine the potential for destruction of which we are now capable. Finally, as I recognized more than once in the course of preparing this text, I am fully aware that not everyone agrees on all these issues. Some, in fact, hold very strong and considered opinions contrary to my own, and I certainly don't pretend to have all the answers to their questions.

This latter point is important to bring up once more. While recognizing divergent points of view, as cited above, all the way back in 2001, the United States Conference of Catholic Bishops mentioned a scientific consensus on which I would rely in their statement *Global Climate*

Afterword

Change: A Plea for Dialogue, Prudence, and the Common Good: "As Catholic bishops, we make no independent judgment on the plausibility of 'global warming.' Rather, we accept the consensus findings of so many scientists and the conclusions of the Intergovernmental Panel on Climate Change (IPCC) as a basis for continued research and prudent action."[37] Much more recently, in *Laudate Deum*, Pope Francis answered objections to the scientific findings on manmade climate change:

> In recent years, some have chosen to deride these facts. They bring up allegedly solid scientific data, like the fact that the planet has always had, and will have, periods of cooling and warming. They forget to mention another relevant datum: that what we are presently experiencing is an unusual acceleration of warming, at such a speed that it will take only one generation—not centuries or millennia in order to verify it.[38]

My contribution to the discussion is to put the topic in a biblical perspective, and this was done most particularly with a focus on the wonders and beauty of the world created by God, and the recurring theme of stewardship of God's creation. The Bible is full of texts that speak of the magnificence of what God has done in forming the planet and all life upon it. In this regard, the Bible is also clear that the world belongs not to us, who are the crowning creation of life on this earth, but to the God who made us as a part thereof and charged us to care for what he has made.

Afterword

So how do we move forward? If we take the idea of stewardship of creation seriously, we can start as individuals. We can try to be more conscious of how we personally treat the environment. Several times above, I have mentioned recycling efforts. That is a nice place to begin. Each of us can do our own part to try to leave this world a little cleaner, a little less polluted, in order to hand something better on to those who follow us. In order to be really effective, though, we need to move beyond individual efforts. As suggested above, looking into and getting involved with efforts in one's parish (or with other nearby faith communities), neighborhood, or municipality is a good way to move beyond the individual to something even more substantial and effective.

As an example, in the introduction, I wrote about Fr. Thomas Berry, C.P., and his advocacy for the environment. In Jamaica, Queens, his religious congregation, the Passionists, has reopened the Bishop Molloy Retreat Center and renamed it The Thomas Berry Place. A good deal of the ethos of the new center is based on the theories of Fr. Berry. Among the improvements to the complex are a retreat house farm which grows fresh produce that is used to feed both community members and guests at the center. In addition, solar panels now create a complete clean energy offset for both The Thomas Berry Place retreat center and the Passionist monastery. Initiatives of this sort go beyond the individual and are another excellent move in the right direction.

I have also mentioned that the more serious problems with the environment and its degradation are beyond our

Afterword

individual control and, I should add, our local collective control. In the last chapter, we reflected on the idea of a social dimension to our stewardship that should be extended particularly for the biggest problems such as climate change, even to national and international levels. Without question, this is the most challenging "answer" to the question of how to live out our stewardship of creation. At these levels, there are powerful interests that would work against our best efforts to help to confront environmental problems and search for a solution. The best we can hope to do in this regard is to utilize our voice and, when possible, our vote. And, of course, we must always rely on the power of prayer; we must pray with all sincerity and regularity that the hearts and minds of people today will be inspired to do everything possible to ensure the good stewardship of God's good creation. Will it at times seem futile? Unfortunately, this is likely. But is it worth the effort? If we take seriously the call to "till and keep" God's creation, then any effort to answer this call and prove ourselves responsible, faithful stewards is worth it.

Notes

1. See https://cup.columbia.edu/book/thomas-berry/9780231176989 (accessed June 15, 2020).
2. "dominion," *Merriam-Webster,* https://www.merriam-webster.com/dictionary/dominion (accessed June 6, 2020).
3. "subdue," *Merriam-Webster,* https://www.merriam-webster.com/dictionary/subdue (accessed June 6, 2020).
4. Pope Francis, *Laudate Deum,* number 25. https://www.vatican.va/content/francesco/en/apost_exhortations/documents/20231004-laudate-deum.html (accessed October 14, 2023).
5. Kashmira Gander, "What Do Evangelical Christians Really Think About Climate Change?," *Newsweek,* September 19, 2019, https://www.newsweek.com/what-evangelical-christians-think-climate-change-1459927 (accessed June 9, 2020).
6. Lisa Vox, "Why Don't Christian Conservatives Worry about Climate Change? God," *Washington Post,* June 2, 2017, https://www.washingtonpost.com/posteverything/wp/2017/06/02/why-dont-christian-conservatives-worry-about-climate-change-god/ (accessed June 2, 2020).
7. Pope Francis, *Laudato Si'* (Città del Vaticano: Libreria Editrice Vaticana, 2015), number 67.
8. *Laudato Si',* number 12.
9. *Laudate Deum,* number 1.
10. *Laudato Si',* number 2.
11. Jerry A. Nathanson, "pollution, environment," Britannica, last updated May 21, 2024, https://www.britannica.com/science/pollution-environment (accessed June 26, 2021).
12. Mark Z. Jacobson, *Air Pollution and Global Warming: History, Science, and Solutions* (Cambridge: Cambridge University Press, 2012), 74.

Notes

13. "Water and Air Pollution," History.com Editors, November 6, 2009 (updated March 30, 2020), https://www.history.com/topics/natural-disasters-and-environment/water-and-air-pollution (accessed August 15, 2021).
14. *Laudate Deum,* number 10.
15. See "Air pollution," Bill Kovarik, Environmental History, https://environmentalhistory.org/about/airpollution/ (accessed August 15, 2021).
16. See John Misachi, "Rivers That Have Caught On Fire," World Atlas, April 25, 2017, https://www.worldatlas.com/articles/is-the-cuyahoga-river-the-only-river-to-ever-catch-on-fire.html (accessed June 29, 2021).
17. St. Clement, *Letter to the Corinthians*, 20. Taken from the Liturgy of the Hours, Office of Readings, Thirtieth Sunday of Ordinary Time.
18. Sara Gorman and Jack M. Gorman, "Climate Change Denial: Facing a Reality Too Big to Believe," *Psychology Today,* January 12, 2019, https://www.psychologytoday.com/us/blog/denying-the-grave/201901/climate-change-denial (accessed June 2, 2022).
19. United States Conference of Catholic Bishops, *Global Climate Change: A Plea for Dialogue, Prudence, and the Common Good,* June 15, 2001, https://www.usccb.org/resources/global-climate-change-plea-dialogue-prudence-and-common-good (accessed March 3, 2022).
20. *Laudato Si',* number 23.
21. *Laudate Deum,* number 2.
22. See Christopher Flavelle, "As the Great Salt Lake Dries Up, Utah Faces an 'Environmental Nuclear Bomb,'" *The New York Times,* June 7, 2022 (updated June 22, 2023), https://www.nytimes.com/2022/06/07/climate/salt-lake-city-climate-disaster.html (accessed June 10, 2022).
23. *Laudato Si',* number 220.
24. *Laudate Deum,* number 62.

25. See Anna Berrill et al, "50 Simple Ways to Make Your Life Greener," *The Guardian*, February 29, 2020, https://www.theguardian.com/environment/2020/feb/29/50-ways-to-green-up-your-life-save-the-planet (accessed May 4, 2023).
26. See Perry Santanachote, "10 Quick Tips for Going Green at Home," Consumer Reports, updated April 22, 2024, https://www.consumerreports.org/environment-sustainability/tips-for-going-green-at-home-a6852276649/ (accessed May 4, 2023).
27. See Mark Kinver, "Then and Now: Pandemic Clears the Air," BBC News, May 31, 2021, https://www.bbc.com/news/science-environment-57149747 (accessed July 14, 2023).
28. UN Environment Program, "Nature Can Still Heal Itself, If We Give It the Urgent Attention It Needs," August 8, 2019, https://www.unep.org/news-and-stories/story/nature-can-still-heal-itself-if-we-give-it-urgent-attention-it-needs (accessed July 18, 2023).
29. *Laudato Si'*, number 190.
30. Darcy Larum, "What Is Fallow Ground: Are There Any Benefits of Fallowing Soil," last updated March 4, 2021, https://www.gardeningknowhow.com/garden-how-to/soil-fertilizers/what-is-fallow-ground.htm (accessed July 20, 2023).
31. *Laudate Deum*, number 27.
32. R. Robert Creech, "'A Sower Went Out to Sow': An Agrarian Reading of the New Testament," *American Baptist Quarterly* 58 (2016), 22–38, here 32.
33. "steward," Merriam-Webster, https://www.merriam-webster.com/dictionary/steward (accessed July 29, 2023).
34. *Laudato Si'*, number 116.
35. *Laudate Deum*, number 69.
36. *Laudate Deum*, number 70.
37. United States Conference of Catholic Bishops, *Global Climate Change: A Plea for Dialogue, Prudence, and the Common Good.*
38. *Laudate Deum*, number 6.

FOCOLARE MEDIA
Enkindling the Spirit of Unity

The New City Press book you are holding in your hands is one of the many resources produced by Focolare Media, which is a ministry of the Focolare Movement in North America. The Focolare is a worldwide community of people who feel called to bring about the realization of Jesus' prayer: "That all may be one" (see John 17:21).

Focolare Media wants to be your primary resource for connecting with people, ideas, and practices that build unity. Our mission is to provide content that empowers people to grow spiritually, improve relationships, engage in dialogue, and foster collaboration within the Church and throughout society.

Visit www.focolaremedia.com to learn more about all of New City Press's books, our award-winning magazine *Living City*, videos, podcasts, events, and free resources.

www.ingramcontent.com/pod-product-compliance
Lightning Source LLC
Chambersburg PA
CBHW072201100426
42738CB00011BA/2493